YO-BCE-435

COUNTY OF DURHAM
NEVILLE'S CROSS
COLLEGE
EDUCATION COMMITTEE.

ABOUT THE BIBLE

ABOUT THE BIBLE

by

FRANK W. MOYLE

BS
538
.M67

LONDON
GEOFFREY BLES
MCMLVI

1956

Printed in Great Britain by
The Pitman Press, Bath
for the publishers
Geoffrey Bles Ltd
52 Doughty Street London WC1

First published 1956

The Library
INTERNATIONAL CHRISTIAN
GRADUATE UNIVERSITY

CONTENTS

36769

"The Lord hath more Truth yet
to bring forth from His
Holy Word."

John Robinson,
Pastor to the Pilgrim Fathers
17th century

"We look to Thee, O Lord; to give us the
fellowship of that Spirit who guided
the Prophets and Apostles, that we
may take their words in the sense
in which they spoke, and assign
its right shade of meaning to
every utterance, for of Thee,
O Father Eternal, and
through Thy Spirit
did they speak."

Hilary
Bishop of Poitiers
4th century
(De Trinitate)

INTRODUCTION

THE Bible was once every Englishman's book. The dreams of those who first gave it to us in English were fulfilled in the seventeenth, eighteenth and even on into the nineteenth century, "that the husbandman might sing it at his plough and the weaver at his shuttle," and that "the boy that drives the plough in England shall know more of Scripture than the Pope does."

But today, though most people still have a copy of it in their houses, they seldom or never refer to it. If one should happen to ask for it, as I often do, it is nowhere to be found. Now and again in a cottage there is a cumbersome old family Bible which scatters dust in all directions if you open it; or in a villa or flat one may catch the glint of its gilt edges closely confined in an elastic band behind the glass doors of the cabinet which is hardly ever opened. More often still it lies somewhere on a lower shelf beneath a pile of "weeklies."

For most people, the one time "Book of Books" has become the book that remains on the shelf. But over against all that, and the general indifference to Religion which is largely responsible for so much ignorance and misunderstanding of the Bible, there are signs of a revival of interest in it. *The Times* recently published a thirty-page supplement to which some of the foremost scholars of the day contributed articles on the historical, social and literary aspects of the Old and New Testaments. This led to a large number of letters in the correspondence column, under the title "The Book of Books," which has shown the need for a less technical and more popular treatment of this great subject for the ordinary reader. I will quote an extract from a long letter which came to me privately the day after a letter of mine had appeared in *The Times*.

". . . I regret that I cannot see the point of your remarks unless they are to discredit Holy Scripture. The Bible carries its own credentials and needs no support from man. . . . I have no difficulty with the literal interpretation of Scripture. If God says a thing, it must be true, because God says it. God cannot lie. I know that the present Creation, as we know it, was called into

vii

being in six days; that the deluge came and destroyed all except those with Noah; that the Children of Israel walked through the Red Sea and through the Jordan as though on dry land; that the sun stood still for a day, etc., etc. I know all these things just because God says so. I care not what man says—'Let God be true and every man a liar'."

From this and from other letters which were published at the time, it is clear that there are still quite a number of folk who would claim that the Bible is not simply the Word but the very words of God and therefore infallible. Indeed, one still meets them. They will tell you that the Bible says this or the Bible says that and there's an end of it. But unfortunately it is not the end of it. That view has had many tragic consequences in our history. Right on into the middle of the eighteenth century, for instance, many innocent persons who displayed unusually developed psychic powers were burnt as witches because "the Bible says, 'Thou shalt not suffer a witch to live'."

A great deal of the opposition to William Wilberforce's Bill for the abolition of slavery came from religious people who were prepared to maintain that slavery is not wrong because the Bible does not forbid it and St. Paul sent back a runaway slave to his master.

We were reminded the other night of another incident which illustrates the harm that has been done by taking the Bible literally, through a radio play on the life of Dr. James Young Simpson. When this great man had discovered chloroform and began to use it as an anaesthetic, he was criticised by devout persons who asserted that he was "going against the Bible," because the legend of Genesis affirms that the Lord God intended women to suffer pain in childbirth. Simpson, however, was able to answer them by replying that in the same passage we are told that it was the Lord God Himself who discovered and applied anaesthetics, for God "caused a deep sleep to fall upon Adam" before extracting the rib out of which He made the first woman. We are not always as fortunate as Doctor Simpson in being able to reply to literal-minded people on their own level.

Introduction

But there is another consequence of the view, which brings me to the main purpose of this book. One can hardly blame the ordinary man, who very seldom applies as much common sense to his religion as he does to his business, if he says, "Either it's true or it isn't," and puts his Bible back on the shelf. Dealing, as he is, with what we call "hard facts" all day long, he is easily led to think that it is only truth of fact which matters, but, as I hope to show, the Bible contains comparatively little in the way of hard facts and much more in the way of the eternal truths by which men have lived. It is to some of those truths that I want to draw the reader's attention. In a book of this size it is impossible to do more than to sketch the main features of Biblical literature, to remove perhaps a few misunderstandings and to show the relevance of the message of some of its books to our human situation at the present time.

In offering these pages to the public, I am painfully aware of my limitations. It has been impossible, during the thirty years of Parish work since I sat at the feet of those who introduced me to Biblical criticism, to keep pace with the ever-changing currents of academic opinion. I am not, however, unaware that some of the conclusions which I was then taught to regard as axiomatic have been modified or even superseded in some instances, particularly with regard to the Old Testament. But I am still more acutely conscious that the gap between the specialists and the man or woman in the pew or in the pub has widened into a great gulf. It is that gulf which I am here attempting to bridge. It will no doubt be quite easy for the academic critic to take me to task on many points where my scholarship is at fault in the light of the latest learned opinion.

It may even be a simple matter for some of them to treat me as Samuel treated Agag, the King of the Amalekites, and "hew me in pieces." But, like poor Agag, I have tried to "tread delicately" on doubtful ground, and it may be that after they have done with me and crumbled this little slice of plain bread into fragments, the plain man for whom I have the most special concern may be able to gather up a crumb or two from what remains!

Allesley, Coventry, 1955   F. W. M.

Approximate Dates of Some of the
Old Testament Writings

B.C.

12th Century   Early songs, probably handed down by *Oral Tradition*:
Song of Deborah and Barak (Judges 5).
Song of Lamech (Genesis 4: 23–24).

11th Century   Song of Joshua (Joshua 10: 12), quoted from an ancient collection called *The Book of Jashar*.
Lament of David over Saul and Jonathan (II Sam. 1), quoted from the same collection.

10th Century   A few early psalms, e.g. Psalm 18.

9th Century   Historical books. Samuel and Kings. (Begun)

8th Century   Amos, Hosea, Micah and Isaiah 1–39.

7th Century   Book of Deuteronomy and Jeremiah published under Josiah 621 B.C.

6th Century   *Period of the Exile 597–538 B.C.*
Much editing of the Early Books.
Later Psalms.
Ezekiel.

5th Century   ⎧ Priestly writers at work (e.g. Genesis 1).
4th Century   ⎨ Ezra, Nehemiah, Book of Job.
  ⎩ Isaiah 40–55. Books of Ruth and Jonah.

3rd Century   Book of Ecclesiastes.

2nd Century   Book of Daniel (165 B.C. during the war with Antiochus).
Completion of the Book of Psalms.

A.D.

1st Century   Closing of the Old Testament Canon of Scripture (Council of Jamnia).

ACKNOWLEDGEMENTS

I should like to express my thanks to Messrs. Hodder & Stoughton Ltd. for their permission to quote from Dr. Moffatt's translation of the Bible, and also to Mrs. George Bambridge, Messrs. Methuen & Co. Ltd. and the Macmillan Company of Canada Ltd. for permission to quote on pages 173 and 174 the lines from *The Years Between* by Rudyard Kipling.

F. W. M.

CHAPTER ONE

Why Read the Bible and How?

THE Sunday after the church of which I was vicar had been destroyed by enemy action in 1941, the landlord of the "local" just up the road invited me to come and meet his customers.

They had already been sending round the hat, and in one week had raised about £30 towards the re-building of the church. After thanking them in the Bar, the Smoke Room, and out on the terrace by the Grand Union Canal, I reminded them that the Founder of the Faith for which we were fighting was born in the stable of an inn and that on the night before he made his supreme sacrifice he said goodbye to his friends in the Upper Room of another.

That episode led to a weekly visit every Sunday night until I left the parish two years later. On my arrival the landlord would rap loudly on the bar-counter and say, "Here's our Vicar, Ladies and Gentlemen. He has a message from God for us." They used to expect an eight to ten minutes' talk. This led, of course, to questions which often kept us going until closing time. One of their first questions was this:

> "Where do we come from,
> Where are we going to,
> And how do you get there?"

There was no time to think, for the questioner added, "that's a quicky, Sir!" Fortunately, the words "do we come" suggested to me the lines from Wordsworth's "Intimations of Immortality":

> "Not in entire forgetfulness,
> And not in utter nakedness,
> But trailing clouds of glory do we come
> From God, who is our home."

So I just said, "We come from God, who is our home." I then went on to suggest that the only adequate answers to these great

3

questions are to be found in the Bible, for it is with questions of just that sort that the Bible is most concerned. That doesn't mean, of course, that the Bible is the sort of book in which you can look up a question and find the answer, though one still occasionally meets people who treat it in that sort of way.

An old lady whom I once knew did. She kept by her bedside a little box which was divided into a number of small cylindrical compartments each containing a tightly rolled piece of paper upon which was found a verse picked indiscriminately from the Bible. If one had followed the advice thus offered, it might have led to the most surprising results. That and similar methods of familiaris-ing people with the contents of the Bible have nothing to recom-mend them. You cannot treat the Bible as though it were a single book. Actually there are thirty-nine different books in the Old Testament and twenty-seven in the New, and since they come to us from a period which covers more than a thousand years and several single books contain the works of several different authors, it would be absurd to expect to make sense of a single sentence apart from the whole passage in which it occurs. And worse still, you would be almost sure to give it your meaning instead of that of the author. No, we must realise from the start that the Bible is not a book but a library containing many books of different kinds. But that needs a word of explanation. If you go to your public library you will always find that the various books are properly classified. So if you found a book of poems on the shelf labelled "Science" you would know that it had got into the wrong place. Or if you found the works of Shakespeare or Milton on the shelf labelled "History," you would never dream of reading *Hamlet* or *Paradise Lost* as history. Unfortunately that is exactly the kind of mistake people have made in reading the Bible, because its books are not classified. But there is a further complication. The Authorised Version of the Bible is divided up into separate little verses, so that the uninstructed reader cannot tell whether he is supposed to be reading prose or poetry. All sorts of difficulties have arisen from reading poetry as prose, or even poetry as science.

The English Scholars who gave us the Revised Version in 1881 have done a great deal to clear up this difficulty by substituting the paragraph for the verse divisions and by printing what is obviously a poem in couplets to distinguish it from prose. This is very important, for example, in the case of Joshua's injunction to the Sun and Moon to stand still. Look at Joshua 10. We are reading a prose narrative: "Then spake Joshua to the Lord in the day when the Lord delivered up the Amorites before the children of Israel." Then suddenly we find ourselves reading what is obviously a fragment of a very ancient poem: "And Joshua said in the sight of Israel,

> *Sun, stand thou still upon Gibeon;*
> *And thou, Moon, in the valley of Ajalon.*
> *And the Sun stood still, and the Moon stayed,*
> *Until the people had avenged themeslves upon their*
> *   enemies."*

The editor of the book of Joshua leaves us in no doubt that it is a fragment of a very ancient poem or war song, because he immediately acknowledges its source—"Is not this written in the Book of Jashar?" We have no record of the "Book of Jashar," but the quotation indicates that this writer had access to a collection of war songs, so named, which has not survived.

The recognition of this little passage as ancient poetry would have saved literal-minded readers like my correspondent (whose remarks I quoted in the Introduction) from feeling bound to accept it as a fact "because the Bible says so." "The Bible" says nothing. Its different authors expressed what they wished to say in different ways; sometimes through facts in prose; sometimes through feelings in poetry, for poetry is the language of excited feeling. What the unknown poet was really trying to say was that the Hebrew warriors enjoyed following up their glorious victory so much that it seemed to them that the hours of daylight had been extended in their favour and that the day would never end. We find just the same kind of thing in another of these ancient poems called "The Song of Deborah and Barak," which celebrated another victory, when "the stars in their courses fought against Sisera" (Judges 5: 20). In the same way, the moment that you realise that the story of the Creation in Genesis 1 is a poem and not science, all the difficulties which led to the bitter controversy between Science and Religion a century ago disappear. The Chapter ought to be headed "A HYMN OF CREATION." There is no such thing as science, as we know it, anywhere in the Bible. All its authors, of the Old and New Testament alike, thought that the earth was a flat disc suspended in space and that Heaven over-arched it like a dish-cover, and that Hell (or the Abyss) yawned beneath it like a cellar. Science, which has taught us that the earth is a small planet of a minor star in the Milky Way and that there is no Heaven above the bright blue sky, was not born till the sixteenth century of our era. Therefore it is very mistaken to try an uphold Biblical views of the Universe against modern science or to imagine that in so doing one is defending the truth of the Bible. The Biblical authors were concerned with quite a different kind of truth. They were not trying to explain *how* the earth and the world were made, but *why*. Surely that is a more important kind of truth. When it comes to the actual living of life, it is more important to know *why* we are here than to be fully acquainted with the details of *how* we came here.

"Where do we come from?" asked the man in the pub. The ancient poet of Genesis 1 would have agreed with his brother poet William Wordsworth, centuries later, in saying, "We come from God." But of course he could only put it in his own way: "So God created man in his own image, in the image of God created he him; male and female created he them."

Nothing that modern science has told us about evolution and the ascent of man who, as Darwin said, "bears in his body the indelible marks of his humble origin," affects in any way the poet's truth. And in fact the ancient poet and the modern scientist are agreed in believing that man is the crown of creation. There is another very important truth in the Hymn of Creation which will have to be borne in mind in the atomic age, if mankind is not to become the victim of his scientific discoveries. It is clearly stated that man, "made in the image of God" (that is, man as a spiritual being), is responsible for the direction and control of all other living things. "*And God said, Let them* (the human race) *have dominion over the fish of the sea . . . and over every creeping thing that creepeth upon the earth"* (Genesis 1 : 26). It is surely of the utmost importance to the human race today that this "Dominion," or intelligent control, should be established over atomic energy. The scientist will say that it is his business to discover these things, but that it is no concern of his to what use they are to be put. To say that is to divorce science from religion and to deny one's responsibility as a spiritual being. Religion without science is lame, but science without religion is blind. Science can supply the tools but religion alone can supply the light which we need to use them rightly, for the benefit and not for the destruction of the human race. The Hymn of Creation in Genesis 1 has a refrain which comes all the way through, as one thing after another is made:

"And God saw that it was good" . . .
*"And God saw everything that he had made, and, behold, it was
   very good."*

If it is to remain good, man must always maintain his relationship with the God who made both him and it. If he severs his connection with God, things are bound to go wrong. That is the truth with which the second and third chapters of Genesis are really dealing. It has become clear to Biblical scholars that these two chapters come from a much earlier period than the first, for they contain a view of the creation which is much more primitive than that of the author of the Hymn of Creation. In the view of the author of Chapters 2 and 3, Man was created before the animals and it was only when the "Lord God" had been unsuccessful in finding a suitable companion for man among the animals that he extracted a rib from Adam's side and out of it created woman, as "an help meet for him." But these childish and picturesque ideas, which are closely akin to the Greek idea of Athena springing fully armed from the head of Zeus, do not invalidate the truth which is contained in the myth of Genesis. It is very important indeed to state clearly that all the first eleven chapters of Genesis belong to this mythical type of literature and that they must be read as folk-tales and not as facts. But that need not prevent us from finding in them certain important moral truths, which an age

7

pre-occupied with science is now in great danger of missing. Look again at the familiar story of the Garden of Eden and you cannot help seeing that the author of this story (which is only the Hebrew version of stories familiar throughout the whole ancient world), though he may have been in our view woefully ignorant of human origins, had profound insight into human nature. He is offering us his answer to the question which has never yet been satisfactorily answered, "Where does evil come from and why is there suffering in the world?" He cannot give a complete answer but is content to tell us what he has learnt from his own observation. He puts what he has to say in the form of a story or myth (the word "myth" is the Greek muthos—a story). Adam (in Hebrew, Man) is rebuked for eating the fruit of the tree of the knowledge-of-good-and-evil which he has been forbidden to eat. He says that his wife persuaded him to eat it and that therefore she is to blame. Eve (in Hebrew, Life) is rebuked for her part in the disobedience, and she puts the blame on the serpent. The poor serpent is dumb! This is surely the author's way of saying that he has traced evil back as far as he can and that he has nothing more to say. But has he not said something of importance? When wrong has been done and suffering follows for innocent people, can we ever find out who is ultimately to blame? Has it not taxed the ingenuity of all the law courts of all the ages to find "the nigger in the wood pile?" And then, when we think we have found him, we can't always be certain unless he confesses his crime. Witnesses may be misinformed or false. We try next to make the punishment fit the crime, but long experience has shown that punishment does not necessarily cure the evildoer, unless he can be induced to accept the responsibility and repent.

That is what this ancient writer has to say, and we can hardly improve the moral or adorn the tale. Jesus Christ endorsed the story, without quoting it, when he said that most of the evil in the world comes not from the world without but from the world within—"out of the heart of man." There is much evil and suffering in the world which still remains to be explained, but there is much more which can be. Rudyard Kipling has said this in his poem "Natural Theology," in which he shows man blaming God for all those troubles and tragedies which man has brought upon himself by his own ignorance, folly and sin. Of about 90 per cent of human misery, Kipling declares,

> "This was none of the Lord's good pleasure;
> For the Spirit He breathed in man is free,
> And what comes after is measure for measure
> And not a God that afflicteth thee.
> As was the sowing, so is the reaping;
> Is now and evermore shall be.
> Thou art delivered to thine own keeping;
> Only thyself hath afflicted thee."

But are we in fact entirely delivered to our own keeping? According to Kipling, "Yes," but according to the Biblical writers, "No, not entirely."

Here is the greatness of the Bible. Its authors are quite emphatic in affirming the truth about human responsibility and saying that we must take the consequences of our sins. But they all with one voice have something even more important to say. They affirm that God does not entirely leave us to our own devices. The early writers of the story of the Flood or the Tower of Babel gave rather a crude picture of God intervening in human affairs. That was because, at the time in which they wrote, men thought of God in terms of the worst and not of the best qualities in human nature. But that was better than the Greeks, who taught that the gods dwelt in a sacred everlasting calm untroubled by human suffering. The Biblical writers were the first to conceive of the Divine concern and compassion and mercy.

> *"There is mercy with Thee, therefore shalt thou be feared . . .*
> *The Lord is full of compassion and mercy, long-suffering and of great goodness. He will not alway be chiding, neither keepeth he his anger for ever. He hath not dealt with us after our sins nor rewarded us according to our wickednesses."*

We may feel sometimes that the Old Testament writers do not do full justice to the freedom of the human will, and tend to over-emphasise the power and majesty of God almost to the point of arbitrariness. But this again is due to the fact, as we shall see later, that it took a long time for the individual as a free responsible human being to emerge from the totalitarianism of the tribal community. Even so advanced a thinker as the prophet Jeremiah still talked of man as clay in the hands of the potter. But it is to the everlasting honour of the Biblical writers that they were able to show, through the history of their nation, that however far man may stray from the path of goodness and truth, and however terrible the disasters man may bring upon himself by his own stupidity and perversity, God never gives him up. More than that, it is always God who takes the initiative in winning men back to the knowledge of Himself. The picture which Jesus painted, of the father who saw his prodigal son "when he was yet a great way off, and had compassion and ran and fell on his neck and kissed him," was there in embryo, as it were, in the Hebrew mind ages and ages before. Hosea, as we shall see presently, heard God saying, "How shall I give thee up?" So I suggest that the Biblical writers have a very important answer to give to the third question of the man in the pub, which was "How do you get there?" How do we get back to "God, who is our home"? The achievements of Science in our day have been so vast and so varied, and have so greatly added to the amenities of life, that we can easily be deceived into thinking that the scientists have a monopoly of Truth. The scientist has taught us to think of man as the seeker, the discoverer and the inventor. So he is, but that is only one side of the truth. It needs to be balanced by the thought of the Biblical writers who tell of the Hand that has guided man and "taught him to walk," of the Mind that has progressively declared unto man the thoughts of God, and of the Spirit which "comes upon him" and has inspired him in his strivings after the good life and shall eventually be "poured out upon all flesh," so that each individual man, woman, and child shall know and love him.

The God whom man has been seeking has been seeking him all the way through. And it is the Spirit of God Himself who guides man to Himself.

Finally, the Bible as expounded by modern scholars shows that man's knowledge of God has come to him, like all his other knowledge, slowly and gradually.

It begins with the picture of a less than half civilised tribe cowering in terror at the foot of Mount Sinai, which they believed to be the abode of the storm-god whose voice was thunder. It ends with the picture of men and women living constructive and joyous lives in the power of that Spirit which dwells not in mountains or even in temples but in the hearts of those who are learning to worship him through their dedicated lives, "in spirit and in truth."

It begins with the picture of Moses meting out laws to a half-civilised people and patiently teaching them the law of limited, instead of unlimited, revenge—one eye for one eye; one tooth for one tooth. It ends with the prayer of Jesus for his murderers, "Father, forgive them; for they know not what they do," and the witness of those who, inspired by him, have learned to "love their enemies and do good to them that hate them."

It begins with the idea that there is nothing after death and that there is "no wisdom or knowledge or device in the grave whither thou goest." It ends with the truth that "we have passed out of death into life, because we love the brethren," and that death is but the gate of life immortal and no human mind can conceive of the wonders which God has in store for his children.

The progress has been slow and uneven and never automatic, but it has been sure, because God has guided it without ever forcing the pace and has inspired man without ever violating his free will to disobey or thwart Him. The progress has been painful, but the pain has not been all on Man's side. God is shown to be "afflicted in the afflictions of his people" and at last through Christ to have "seen the travail of his soul and to have been satisfied," and to have taken upon Himself the whole responsibility.

That is the kind of answer which can be made in defence of the Bible against modern writers, like Mr. Fred Hoyle, who seem inclined to claim a monopoly of truth and to be unwilling to admit that there can be any kind of truth other than scientific truth. "Is it reasonable," he wrote in his recent book, "to suppose that it was given to the Hebrews to understand mysteries far deeper than anything I can comprehend, when it is quite clear that they were completely ignorant of many things that seem commonplace to me?" (*The Nature of the Universe*, by Fred Hoyle. Basil Blackwell).

Is it not possible that Mr. Hoyle and others have become so absorbed with the question "How?", which is the scientific problem, that they have completely lost sight of the question "Why?", which is the religious problem? That may have a serious effect upon their personalities and in the end a fatal effect upon the life of man on this planet. If man allows himself to forget why he is here, he is quite likely to become the victim of that frame of mind which "couldn't care less." And that spells suicide. Man needs not only bread—material amenities—to strengthen his heart, but a wisdom higher than his own to inform his heart, to inspire his will and to direct his spirit. So Charles Darwin confessed in his autobiography, and he may be regarded as one of the fathers of modern science. In his old age, Darwin tells us that if he could have his life over again he would spend at least an hour a week listening to great music or reading great poetry. Why? He says that he would find time for these pursuits because his neglect of them seems to have had an "injurious effect" upon his character. He can, he admits, no longer read Shakespeare or listen to music or even enjoy beautiful scenery, because his mind seems to have become a "kind of machine for grinding out general laws from large collections of facts."

Well, the Bible is full of great poetry and full of the music of great lives which were lived—and in most cases laid down—in the faith that the strains and stresses, the turmoil and the tribulations of this mortal life will one day be seen to have been worth while, and that through taking the right attitude towards them men and women may reach that spiritual maturity which St. Paul called "the measure of the stature of fullness of Christ."

CHAPTER TWO

The God Who Speaks

You may have heard the story of the little girl who was observed sitting on the floor furiously drawing a picture with coloured crayons on a large sheet of cardboard. Her mother, looking over her shoulder, asked, "What on earth are you trying to draw?" "Can't you see, Mummy," the child replied, "I'm drawing God." "But you can't draw God, darling," said the mother. "Nobody has ever seen God and nobody knows what God is like." The little girl wetted her crayon in her mouth and went on with her picture, replying, "Well, they will when I've finished my picture."

Of course, both the mother and the child were right! As St. John says: "No man hath seen God at any time." And no one in this finite world can ever see God as He is in the infinite glory of his Eternal Being. Even Jesus Christ could not do that. But Christians believe that St. John was quite justified in claiming that Jesus has given us the supreme revelation of God. Jesus Christ knew all that mortal man with his limited human equipment can ever know of God; and his idea, the dominant picture in his mind, was of God as "Our Father"—not just *his* father, but the father of the whole human family. But it is often forgotten that, according to St. John, Jesus qualified all that he had taught about God by saying, "These things have I spoken unto you in parables." A parable is a kind of picture in words. That, of course, immediately reminds us of what is generally admitted to be the greatest picture of God—the father of the Prodigal Son and his elder brother. If we stick to that, we can never go far wrong in our attempts to "picture" God. I should imagine that the Anglican bishops had this in mind when, in their Lambeth Conference of 1930, they said, "Never must our thought of God be inconsistent with all that we may learn of His character in Christ." Not only did Jesus show us a picture of God as Father, but also in his earthly life he actually showed us the kind of way God acts as a father. Now this is very important when we ask the question, "What has the Bible to tell us about God?" It tells us two things which must be kept distinct if we are to think truly of God. For the Bible, especially the Old Testament books, gives us a great many pictures (in words) of God which are quite as childish as the one which the little girl produced with her coloured crayons. That is one thing the Bible gives us. The other thing, which is much more important, is this. The Bible, especially the New Testament books but to some extent also certain parts of the Old Testament, gives us an actual revelation of God which is not due to human imagination (although, of course, God used the imagination of men like Moses and Isaiah and Jeremiah, and Jesus himself, to convey it) but to the revealing activity of God himself.

Perhaps we might compare the Bible in this respect with a coin of the realm, which has two sides. On the obverse is the head of the reigning sovereign which is always the same as long as he lives, and appears on every coin, while the reverse has many different signs which tell you the value of the coin. So with the Bible. The more we study it the more clearly do we come to see what is God's revelation of himself, which is for ever the same (since "The Lord God Omnipotent Reigneth"), and what is man's variable and changing valuation or apprehension of Him. There are two sides to be seen all the time—man's picture of God on the one side, and God's actual revelation of Himself on the other. One of the Psalmists seems to have been aware of this distinction when he wrote, "Truth shall flourish out of the earth: and Righteousness hath looked down from Heaven." We must always look at the Bible the right side up.

Now although we have no doubt whatever that a true revelation of God has come to the human race through the Jews, we must never forget that to begin with they were no different from other primitive peoples. That is why their literature, particularly in the early parts of the Old Testament, reflects so many childish pictures of God. They were, as we all are as children, just like the child who was quite certain that she could draw her picture of God and that when it was finished it would be a true picture. I remember, as a child, being told a great deal by my mother about

an uncle who lived in Australia but whom I was never likely to
see in the flesh. But that did not prevent me from forming a
definite picture of a great broad-shouldered man with a flowing
beard and large strong capable hands, who always wore riding
boots and spurs and carried a couple of loaded revolvers. One day
my mother showed me a photograph of him. I absolutely refused
to believe that it could possibly be that uncle! The photograph
bore no resemblance whatever to the Australian stockrider of my
imagination. It has always been something like that with God;
so that when, as we believe, Jesus came and showed us "the like-
ness of the invisible God," all but a very few absolutely refused to
recognise him. Now the early Hebrews, like everybody else, had
their childish pictures of God as a great big man who "walked
in the garden in the cool of the day" (Gen. 3 : 5) and who had to
take precautions lest man should become too big for his boots and
achieve immortality, and therefore posted an angel with a flaming
sword to bar the way to the "Tree of life" (Gen. 3 : 22). They also
pictured God as a temperamental sort of man like themselves, who
made mistakes and then tried to rectify them. "*And it repented the
Lord that he had made man on the earth, and it grieved him at his
heart; and the Lord said, I will destroy man.*" Hence the Flood! But—
there is nearly always a "but" in these ancient Hebrew stories,
which shows that they had a glimmer of the truth—"*Noah found
grace in the eyes of the Lord*"; that is to say, they *did* think God was a
little better than that and made an exception in the case of a man
who was a bit above the average!

It is these little faint glimmers of light in the primitive Hebrew
stories which makes them more worthy of preservation than
the primitive stories of the gods amongst other nations like the
Babylonians or Egyptians. Here is another instance of this. A well-
known hymn speaks of our heathen forbears "bowing down to
wood and stone." The connection in men's minds between the
Deity and wood and stone or other material things is very ancient
and almost universal, and survives to this day in such strange
customs as "touching wood" or wearing necklaces of precious
stones "for luck," or presenting a newly wedded bride with a
horseshoe. You will remember the famous story of Jacob's

dream, at Bethel, when he took "of the stones of that place for his pillows"? Why not use his knapsack? It would have been much more comfortable! Simply because Jacob believed in the virtue of stones. Superstitious? Yes; but read again the story of his dream and you will find something more than a glimmer of light. Heaven and earth, the unseen and the seen, *connected* by a ladder! Have we as clear a perception of prayer as that? Can we see "the traffic of Jacob's ladder fixt between Heaven and Charing Cross"? There is a truth here in this primitive story!

That brings us to the stories of Moses in the book of Exodus; and in him the glimmers of the light of God's revelation become a positive flame. But before coming to that, it is important to remind the reader of those legendary or mythical elements which we mentioned in Chapter One. Legends do not always belong to the remote past. A great man or woman may become a legend in his or her lifetime. Florence Nightingale, for instance, suffered a great deal of embarrassment from what she called "her legend." It was undoubtedly the same with Moses. All sorts of "wonder stories" must have grown up around him long before his death. It is a certain fact of history that Moses was a great leader and emancipator, lawgiver and teacher, and that he succeeded in leading a horde of undisciplined slaves out of Egypt and welding them into a nation whose significance for the history of mankind increases rather than diminishes with the passage of time. But as to the actual truth about how he did it by bringing plagues on the Egyptians, including the killing off in one night of all their first born, we cannot be so certain. Moses may have been a magician who had a mightier magic than the Egyptians, but I think we should be justified in calling most of that a part of "his legend." Let us say that Moses was the sort of man of whom his contemporaries (who were, we must remember, very crude in their ideas about God) might believe almost anything, and leave it at that. Let us come immediately to what I have called the positive flame of revelation which leaps out at us in the story of the burning bush. Whether or not Moses got some of his ideas about God from the teaching of the great Pharaoh Akhnaton of the fifteenth century B.C., whom we now know to have been the pioneer monotheist

(worshipper of one God only), doesn't very much matter—
although Sigmund Freud in his last book, *Moses and Monotheism*,
makes out a very good case for it, and the possible connection
is profoundly interesting. (Whenever we read the life of a great
discoverer or inventor, we nearly always find that somebody else
had paved the way for him.) What we must not miss as we read
Exodus 3 is the true idea of revelation and inspiration which it
gives. Here is a young shepherd, a fugitive from Egypt where he
had committed murder and whence he had had to run for his life,
burdened and weighed down with the sufferings of his fellow-
countrymen and quite unable to see what he could possibly do to
help. Add to that the fact that he himself could easily have spent
the rest of his life in perfect safety in the house of his father-in-law,
Jethro, the priest of Midian; and then try to dismiss the story of
the burning bush and what came of it as an old yarn with nothing
in it, or as nothing more than a legend or a flight of fancy spun out
of Moses' imagination. The enlightenment which he received
that evening, when his eye was attracted by a scrubby desert bush
lit up in the rays of the setting sun, was so staggering, the conviction that he must somehow emancipate his people and get them
out of Egypt was so irresistible (though we are told that Moses
resisted it at first very strongly), that it cannot have been created
by Moses' own imagination, though God certainly used his
imagination to register it. Just as Jacob's ladder was a true revelation of the connection between the seen and the unseen worlds,
so Moses' bush, lit up but not consumed, is that true revelation of
God speaking to man which we call inspiration—the impact of a
power not ourselves upon our consciousness which brings us a
wisdom higher than our own and a strength which we do not of
ourselves possess. Without that tremendous experience of God
which came to Moses we should never have had his moral code
of the Ten Commandments, which is still the basis of western
jurisprudence. It is particularly significant for our subject in this
chapter that Moses' second commandment forbade the making of
graven images, which was his word of warning against our
inveterate habit of forming false pictures of God in our minds.
We break this commandment whenever we make a god of our

17

country or make a god of sport or speed or science or money, for a man's god is always the thing he cares for most!

A later writer was so enthusiastic about Moses that he said that there had not arisen a prophet "like unto Moses whom the Lord knew face to face," rather suggesting that there never would. Of course he was wrong. The revelation of God to mankind is something gradual and progressive. It goes on age after age. It is going on still. It will be going on a hundred, a thousand, ten thousand years hence. So, as we turn the pages of the Old Testament, it is like watching the dawn over a mountain range. Gradually peak after peak is lit up and more and more of God's nature and character is revealed to the mind of man.

When we come to the eighth century, B.C. the picture is at first sight rather discouraging, almost as discouraging as the picture of the first half of the twentieth century with its two world wars and the threat of the hydrogen bomb. It is a picture of vicious tribal wars, social injustice, widespread immorality, and crass human stupidity as well. Here is the little Jewish nation, now not even one state but divided into two, Judah and Israel, (together occupying a territory no bigger than Wales), after the golden days of David and Solomon still nursing in its imagination a false picture of God. Most of them still imagine that God is to be served by the offering of sacrifices and the punctual observance of feast, fast and ritual, "new moon and sabbath," and that provided these religious exercises are duly performed all will·be well with the nation. They seem to have forgotten all about the Ten Commandments, and they have certainly forgotten the teaching of Moses, that idolatry is the really fatal sin and that morality and fair dealing, justice, and even a little mercy, is what God requires. To make matters worse—and this is where their stupidity came in—they are such shallow optimists, politically, that they just ignore the signs of the times. They are quite oblivious to the hard fact that they are only a little buffer state between two mighty, heavily armed nations—Assyria on the north-east and Egypt on the south-west—who are covetous of the little strip of seaboard, the Philistine coast. And these poor ignorant people suppose that the little national six-foot god of their imagination, as he had become, will save and deliver them, because they have been taught that ever since he brought them up from Egypt they have been and always will be his chosen people. Hardly a promising moment for a new enlightenment or revelation from God! But this was just the moment when it came. To that people steeped in superstition and nearly sunk in immorality through their adoption of the worship of Canaanite nature gods (Baals) came in that eighth century B.C. the greatest spiritual teachers known to history—the Hebrew prophets, Amos, Hosea, Micah, and Isaiah (Ch. 1–39). Each of these men would demand a chapter—or better still, a whole book—to himself, if we were to do them even a little justice, so great is their contribution to the development of our ideas of God; but we must be content here with a summary. They have, of course, long been recognised as paving the way for Christ, but I'm afraid that many people are still put off from reading them by the unfortunate associations which have gathered round the word "prophet." Is he not, to many people still, an emaciated old gentleman with long hair carrying a bundle of Old Moore's Almanacks under his arm? There could not be a more ridiculous caricature. These men are spiritual giants, towering head and shoulders above their contemporaries so that their heads catch the glory of that sunrise of enlightenment which we are still watching as it slowly breaks upon the world. They are the great men of vision without whom the people perish. They were not so much *fore*tellers of the future (though they saw a good deal further into it than most people) as *forth*tellers of the truth about God. Their writings do not make easy reading because they were only very roughly thrown together, probably during the period of the Exile which they could see coming. But we can see the main gist of what they had to say. The great prophets were practical men of affairs. They were not professors or university dons whose work is in the study; they were not authors, in our sense of the word, who made a living out of writing books, but men in ordinary everyday occupations. Amos, the earliest of them, was "an herdman and grower of sycomores"; that is, a rancher and fruit farmer of the yeoman type. Hosea may have been a Cabinet Minister in the government of more than one great king; he was

19

certainly a more educated man, for his writings show that he was a student of history. Isaiah, as is well known, was a statesman whose lightest word on the nation's foreign policy carried as much weight as that of Pitt or Churchill, and who weathered the storm of the Assyrian invasion which swept away Judah's northern neighbour Israel into captivity, and preserved his country's freedom for another hundred years. Micah, who was obviously a peasant, if he had done nothing else has left us with one short sentence which might be taken as a summary of the message common to them all:

"*God hath shewed thee, O man, what is good; and what doth the Lord require of thee, but to do justly, and to love mercy, and to walk humbly with thy God?*"

If we were to single out the special revelation of God which was given through each, we can safely say that "do justly" is Amos' great contribution; "love mercy" represents the more pleading voice of Hosea; and "walk humbly with thy God" might be a fair summary of the call to holiness of life which comes from Isaiah. Righteousness, Mercy, Holiness of life: these are the great requirements of true religion because and simply because God is righteous, God is merciful and God is "the high and holy one who inhabiteth eternity." How then were these great truths about God revealed? They were not revealed through some mystical vision when the prophet was in some sort of trance; they were revealed through the prophets' insight into the meaning of the events and circumstances of their time. This is especially to be seen in the case of Amos. He begins with a tremendous indictment of man's inhumanity to man which he has observed among the heathen nations round about. Syria has shown inhuman conduct towards a conquered foe (1: 3); Gaza has gone in for a cruel slave-trade (1: 5); Tyre has forgotten "the brotherly covenant" (that is, regarded treaties as scraps of paper. (1 : 9)); Edom is guilty of an unbrotherly and unjustifiable continuance of war (1: 11); Ammon has "ripped up the women with child of Gilead, that they might enlarge their border" (1: 13) (that is, in our language, shown frightfulness to women in the interests of imperialism). All that is bad enough, he declares, among the heathen who know no better,

but exactly the same kind of thing is going on in Israel who ought
to. In Israel itself there is nothing but unbrotherly conduct and
social injustice. "They sell the righteous for silver, and the needy
for a pair of shoes" (2: 6). They trample down the poor like dust
(2: 7). And the priests are just as bad. They encourage drunken-
ness that they may grow fat on fines (2: 8); they allow immorality
in the temple itself (just as they did in heathen temples in India)
(2: 7); and they try to silence the prophet who reproves them
(2: 12). Do they really think that a righteous God is going to over-
look all this just because they keep up a hollow show of religiosity
with their feasts and fasts and sacrifices? No, they have had more
religious education than their heathen neighbours; therefore, since
God is righteous, He will expect a much higher standard from
them—"You only have I known of all the families of the earth:
therefore I will punish you for all your iniquities" (3: 2). In a word,
the greater the religious privileges, the greater the moral responsibilities. So, Amos argues, God the righteous one is no more
likely to protect Israel from the invasion that is coming than the
nations who do not know Him. Amos, then, is the first to proclaim that God deals with mankind not, as they think, by
favouritism or caprice, but according to the laws of an absolutely
just and righteous and incorruptible judge, and that it is only as
we become more righteous and just in our dealings with our
fellowmen that we ourselves become more truly religious people.

The Hebrew prophets are the best illustration of the truth that
God reveals himself in many ways, so we shall not be surprised
to find that a great revelation was made to a contemporary of
Amos in a most strikingly different way. The prophet Hosea, both
in his character and in the nature of the revelation which came to
him, provides us with a total contrast. "The two men," wrote
Professor Robertson Smith, "are types of a contrast which runs
through the whole history of religious thought and life down to
our own days. Men of the type of Amos are often condemned as
rationalists and cold moderates; the school of Hosea are regarded
as enthusiasts and unpractical mystics. But God chose his prophets
from men of both types and preached the same lesson to Israel
through both." Hosea, as I have already mentioned, comes to his

supreme experience of the divine revelation out of a totally different social background to that of Amos. Hosea is a city man and possibly moved in what we should call "high society." If so, the tragedy of his home life, which obviously lies behind his whole message as it has come down to us in the fourteen short chapters of his book, was all the more devastating. In his first three chapters, Hosea does a thing which few other ancient writers (with the possible exception of St. Augustine in his famous *Confessions*) have been brave enough to do: he lifts the veil of his private life and shows his scars. He had married a woman named Gomer. At first they lived happily together, calling their firstborn son Jezreel, a name of great promise meaning "of God's sowing" or "God will sow," thereby suggesting hope for the nation which Amos had lost hope of. But just when his wife was expecting their second child, Hosea discovered that she had been unfaithful to him and that the child about to be born was hers but not his. He called the little girl Lo-ruhamah, which means "one that knew not a father's love" or, as Dr. Moffatt translates it, "No-mercy." A third child was born, a son this time, to whom Hosea gave the terrible name Lo-ammi, which means "No child of mine." After that his wife left him and, as he says," went after her lovers." Through all this and even after she had left him for other men, Hosea still yearned after her, never losing hope that some day he would win her back. How many months or years he waited we don't know, but at last one day Hosea decided to go in search of his wife. One can well imagine the kind of counsel his friends would give him in days when it was the easiest thing in the world for a man to divorce his wife, but Hosea did not listen to them. Instead he seems to have paid heed to the tenderness which he still felt in his heart for Gomer, and believed it to be God's way of telling him to go on hoping against hope. So one morning, paying no heed to the shame it might bring on a man of his social standing, he decided to visit the slave market where women were sold to the highest bidder. There, amongst the poor degraded creatures, Hosea saw his wife. His own words tell us the rest: "So I bought her to me for fifteen pieces of silver and eighteen bushels of barley." He took her home and, after a period of probation during which there was no marital relationship, restored her as his wife. That is the experience from which Hosea gives his message to Israel. Like Gomer, Israel has been unfaithful to God—"going after her lovers," the false gods of the heathen—but he seems to hear the very voice of God yearning over His people; *"How shall I give thee up . . . mine heart is turned within me, my compassions are kindled together; I will not return and destroy Ephraim: for I am God, and not man; the Holy One in the midst of thee."*

Hosea thus became one of the pioneers of what we call spiritual experience. He realised, though probably not until it was all over, that all the agony and shame that he had undergone because of his wife's unfaithfulness, and his own tenderness and patience which were born out of it, were but a pale shadow of the agony of God over his faithless people, Israel, whom He had been educating from birth. *"I taught Ephraim to walk, holding them in my arms . . . and I drove them with the harness of love."* Here is his great word Love, or Lovingkindness, which came to him as a direct revelation not only of God's attitude to Israel but as something which he had directly experienced himself in his trouble. It is the first time that we hear that greatest of all words, Lovingkindness (what the New Testament writer called "the tender mercy of God"). Hosea anticipates the teaching of Christ and St. John by saying, in effect, that the only way really to know God is to show lovingkindness to the rest of the family and especially to those who have failed and sinned and let us down. The book of Hosea is one of the most difficult to read because he has woven together the story of his own domestic tragedy with that of the unfaithfulness of his nation. All the same, he has left us two sentences which are little revelations in themselves even when isolated from their context; both were beaten out on the anvil of experience—*"The valley of trouble, a door of hope,"* and, *"I desire mercy* (lovingkindness) *not sacrifice."* The second of these Christ quoted in reply to his critics who objected to his compassion for sinners.

Finally, we have in the writings of Isaiah a revelation of God, again through the prophet's personal experience, which in a sense combines the opposite elements in the teaching of Amos and Hosea. In the experience of his call in the sixth chapter, Isaiah feels

3

at one and the same time both the merciful goodness and the righteous severity of God, in the idea of Holiness.

"Holy, holy, holy is the Lord of hosts:
the whole earth is full of his glory."

So we have now perhaps seen from the literature of the Old Testament some picture or revelation of God gradually unfolding itself in the inspired imagination of man. And it is a revelation of the God who speaks, *"Declaring unto man what is his thought"* (Amos 4: 13).

CHAPTER THREE

The Individual's Response

"WHY is the God of the Old Testament so different from the God of the New?" I once had to try and answer this very important question in a quarter of an hour on the B.B.C. It is indeed one of those very reasonable questions which has always bothered the plain man. And, of course, it is not new. It has not been created by modern scholarship, although it has a modern ring about it. A little more than a hundred years after the death of Christ, in one of those little infant Christian communities at Pontus in Asia Minor, it troubled a certain shipmaster named Marcion so much that he gave up what seemed to him a hopeless conundrum and decided that the Old and New Testaments must have been inspired by two totally different Gods. He got a considerable following, and taught his disciples that the Old Testament scriptures were quite valueless to the Christian reader. I should not be surprised to find that many a Christian layman, even a Christian Churchman, feels much the same. If so, I hope that the previous chapter may have begun to suggest an answer to the difficulty.

A child who had been given something of our present outlook is said to have exclaimed enthusiastically at the end of a Scripture lesson, "How God has improved!" She was on the right track, for although of course God never changes, our ideas about Him have changed very much and are very different from those of the men who wrote the early parts of the Old Testament, or at least from those whose views about God are reflected in books like Judges, Samuel, or Kings. And we can say that on the whole our ideas *have* improved, although false religious ideas take longer to die than any others. We can agree with the New Testament author of the "Letter to the Hebrews" when he begins by saying, "God, who at sundry times and in divers manners spake in time past unto the fathers by the prophets, hath in these last days spoken unto us by his Son." He is the God who speaks. In this chapter we are to consider how the individual can respond to the divine voice.

First we must recognise that, just as man's ideas about God have gone through a long and complicated development, so have man's ideas about himself. This is equally important if we are going to make sense of many things in the Old Testament, and it also has a very special importance for us in our day, when the rights and liberties of the individual are being threatened by the coming of the Totalitarian state. Totalitarianism is an ugly word for an ugly thing. But the trend towards it seems well and truly to have set in. A certain amount of collectivism is, of course, essential in large communities like ours and is extremely convenient. It is much better to be able to use the public water-supply by turning on a tap than to have to pump one's water from the well. It is much more convenient to be able to entrust one's letters to the Post Office than to wait till a trustworthy traveller happens to be going the right way, as St. Paul had to. No one would wish to go back to privately-owned roads with toll gates. But with the coming of the Welfare State, in spite of all its tremendous advantages, the question is bound to arise, as it has already arisen through the coming of the Industrial Revolution and the machine and mass production, as to what effect all this is going to have on personal initiative and the sense of individual responsibility. And when it comes to religion and religious organisations and authoritarian Churches, this question becomes still more pressing. The first item on the agenda of any great assembly of the Church or group of churches ought to be, "What is our present set-up doing to the individual?" But I'm afraid it is more likely to be, "How can we make our Church more powerful and efficient?" If so, we ought to take a long look at Christ and what He had to say about the primary importance of the individual soul, and the clear judgment that He gave about the secondary importance of institutions like the sabbath. ("The sabbath," He said, "was made for man; not man for the sabbath.") But of that, more anon.

I want just now to take you back into Old Testament times to show the kind of things that can happen to the individual in a primitive society which was totalitarian in everything but name, for that is precisely what the ancient Hebrew State was like in the time of David and Solomon. That will help to clear up several misunderstandings about some of the strange and cruel things God is supposed to have done. When the Old Testament writers record that "God said this," or "The Lord said that," we must always take into account the primitive stage of belief about God and Man which had been reached at that particular time.

The instance I shall take is from II Samuel 21. The country had suffered a three years' famine, and we read, "*Year after year David sought the face of the Lord* (that is, consulted the priestly oracle), *and the Lord said* (which means that the oracle gave judgment), "*The guilt of blood lies on Saul and his house, for having slain the Gibeonites.*" That meant that the famine was attributed to God's displeasure at the behaviour of King Saul towards the Gibeonites a generation ago, and that according to the traditional Mosaic belief "the sins of the fathers" had to be visited upon the children "unto the third and fourth generation," so there might yet be more to come! David immediately took action and asked the Gibeonites what they wanted; "*And he said, What ye shall say, that will I do for you.*" The aggrieved Gibeonites had their answer ready: "*The man that consumed us, and that devised against us . . ., let seven men of his sons be delivered unto us, and we will hang them up unto the Lord in Gibeah of Saul.*" David handed over the unfortunate (and innocent) victims—two of Saul's sons and five of his grandsons—to the Gibeonites, who proceeded to execute them. "*And they hanged them in the hill before the Lord . . . and after that, God was intreated for the land.*" It is easy to see from this that the individual had no rights whatever, whenever it was felt that the safety, honour, and welfare of the tribe was at stake. The belief at that time was that God deals with the tribe as a unit and that if famine or any other disaster, such as defeat in battle, overtakes it, it is evident that the Deity has been offended in some way and must be propitiated. It would have been quite beside the point for any of those seven men to have pleaded that they were not responsible for what Saul had done years ago. The priestly oracle regarded them as responsible simply and solely because Saul's blood was in their veins, and their deaths were necessary for reasons of national security. That is a primitive form of totalitarianism. The individual is of no account and has no rights. There are a great many stories in the Old

Testament which reflect the same ideas, and other instances are found in the story of Korah, Dathan, and Abiram, and in the story of Achan, whose family was put to death because he had kept a portion of the loot from the battle of Jericho and so infringed a tribal taboo. As we read them, we must bear in mind that the Israelites at that time believed that a single transgression of any tribal law involved the whole family or kinship group to which the offender belonged. Now let us see how this primitive idea that you were simply a member of a tribe, with no rights or responsibilities as an individual, was gradually superseded.

So long as it was believed that the blessing of God could be secured for the tribe by the performance of specific religious rites, such as the offering of sacrifices, the due observance of festivals and fasts, "new moons and sabbaths," and the strict preservation of tribal taboos, there could be practically no such thing as personal morality in our sense of the word at all. Whatever fair dealing or honesty or purity or mercy there was, would be due to the goodness inherent in human nature as such and to what remained of the authority of the last five of the Ten Commandments which had inculcated it. By the middle years of the eighth century all this was on the wane. It was just then, when morality was at its lowest ebb and the northern kingdom of Israel was rejoicing in a temporary period of material prosperity (always thought to be a sign of the divine favour), that the first great prophet, Amos, arrived. It was he who heralded the new era in which the individual began to become the unit instead of the tribe. Amos taught, as we saw in the previous chapter, that God is righteous and therefore demands from the individual moral behaviour instead of ritualistic performances. This became clearer still in his younger contemporary, Isaiah. His sixth chapter, which is his own account of how he came to be a prophet, gives such a vivid picture of his own personal emancipation from his inherited ideas of God and of himself that it is well worth looking at in some detail. Here indeed we have a sort of "close-up" of the birth of the individual from his primitive tribal background. The long prosperous reign of King Uzziah had ended in tragedy. He had reigned for fifty-two years in Jerusalem and had done much for national defence and agricultural development. We are told that "he loved the soil." But the king had religious ideas which were ahead of his time, and he had clashed with the priests. Going into the Temple one morning, he had tried to assert his right to "burn incense" in the inner sanctuary. Standing across the entrance was the High Priest with eighty members of the order barring his way. The High Priest denounced him for committing an act of sacrilege and for usurping the special privilege of the priestly office. It is said that the King was immediately stricken with leprosy "by the hand of God" and he had to spend the rest of his life in complete isolation and died within a year. This act, and what followed, shook the country. It was interpreted as a sign of the Divine displeasure and the whole nation felt a share in the uncleanness of its leper King. That explains the feelings of the young courtier and rising statesman, Isaiah, when he went into the Temple one day soon after the King's death. *"Woe is me! for I am a man of unclean lips, and I dwell in the midst of a people of unclean lips: for mine eyes have seen the King, the Lord of Hosts."* But as he goes on to tell us of his experience there, one can see that there were other thoughts moving in the mind of Isaiah besides the idea of uncleanness. After all, he thought, had the King been so very wrong in wishing to hold direct communion with God? Was it to be for ever necessary for priests to act as intermediaries between God and man? Could not he, Isaiah, a layman, reach the holy presence directly? But these thoughts were not unmixed with fear. I think that this is what he means to convey when he says, *"the foundations of the threshold shook and the temple began to fill with smoke."* The idea of the awful holiness of God which was supposed to make Him inaccessible to any but specially consecrated priests—that idea upon which the very idea of priesthood stood—all but overwhelmed him as it had evidently and tragically destroyed the King. But not quite. As he tried to ascend in heart and mind to meet God face to face, as it were, God came and met him. It seemed that a veiled presence approached him with *"a live coal in his hand, which he had taken with the tongs from off the altar: and he laid it upon my mouth. and said, Lo, this hath touched thy lips; and thine iniquity is taken away, and thy sin purged."*

Was not this an assurance to Isaiah that God deals directly with man? The "live coal" from the altar coming and touching his mouth was the symbol of direct inspiration as opposed to the indirect declaration of God's will through priestly mediation. Isaiah now knew that he might draw near with faith and confidence, and that brought into his consciousness something more about God than he had ever realised before. Isaiah knew well enough his need of God, but now it flashed across his mind—he says he heard a voice speaking—that God actually needed him. "*And I heard the voice of God saying, Whom shall I send, and who will go for us?*" But is not God omnipotent? Cannot God do everything that he wants to do by himself? Isaiah is the recipient here of a revelation that is still widely ignored in our world; namely, that there is nothing that God can do in the world of human affairs without the intelligent, consecrated, active co-operation of human beings. It was this realisation that led Isaiah to make the great response of the individual: "*Here am I; send me.*" We may have travelled perhaps too far in the opposite direction and fondly imagine that *we* can do all that is necessary towards creating a better world on our own. If so, this picture of the birth of the idea of the importance of the individual and his God-given sense of responsibility would be a healthy corrective.

But it takes a long time for a new idea which has visited the imagination of genius to take root in the common mind. Thomas Carlyle was right when he said that history is the story of what great men have done here: so was Browning when he hinted that God needs a great soul to move men "even to a cleaner sty!" It actually took over a hundred years for the teaching of Isaiah and his fellow prophets, Amos, Hosea and Micah, to affect legislation and get the rights and responsibilities of the individual (as against those of the tribe) acknowledged in a revision of the ancient Mosaic Law. But this eventually came to pass. Here, for once, the mists which enshroud so much of Hebrew history are rolled away, and we can with something like certainty give an actual date to the publication of a new Law Book which, by embodying the teaching of the great prophets, wiped away many of the tribal laws, customs and taboos which had hitherto cramped the style of the individual both in his social and religious life. That book is the one we know as Deuteronomy (incorporated according to Hebrew tradition with the other four "Books of Moses," because like the others it is a law book). It used to be thought, of course, that Moses wrote it, because it appears under his name; but a peep at its last page gives the lie to that, since it contains a description of the death of that great man. But its authors have put the whole of their teaching into the mouth of Moses, the great lawgiver, as though he were still speaking to his people. They were saying in effect, "This is what Moses, your first great teacher and reformer, would be saying to the nation now."

The story of what we should call its "publication" seems to have been preserved for us by the author of II Kings 22. He tells us how in the eighteenth year of King Josiah (621 B.C.), during some repairs to the interior of the Temple, "Hilkiah the High Priest said unto Shaphan the scribe, I have found the book of the law in the house of the Lord." They took it immediately to the King who, having read it "in the ears of all the people," proceeded to carry out a wholesale reformation along the lines laid down in this book of the second (Deutero) or Revised Law. The actual reforms prescribed need not concern us here in any detail. I will only mention one of the most drastic. The local sanctuaries (or parish churches as we should call them), which had been the scene of so much idolatry, immorality and corruption, were closed down. In place of this, the whole male population was to go up to Jerusalem to worship in the Temple three times a year, a practice with which we are familiar six hundred years later in the time of Christ. But the most striking thing about the book of Deuteronomy for our subject in this chapter is the statement of the complete reversal of the ancient teaching of the second Mosaic Commandment about God "visiting the sins of the fathers upon the children unto the third and fourth generation"—a command which had been responsible, as we have seen, for the punishment and death of so many innocent victims, like the sons and grandsons of King Saul. Here is Deuteronomy 24: 16: "*Fathers shall not be put to death for their children, nor children for their fathers: everyone shall be put to death for his own sin.*"

31

This cut clean through the ancient tribal law of inherited or communal guilt and made the individual responsible for his own wrongdoing only. Furthermore, the direct individual approach to God, as opposed to the approach through priestly mediation, is now approved and commanded. "*If you seek the Eternal your God, you shall find Him, provided that you seek for Him with all your mind and all your soul . . . for the Eternal your God is a merciful God; He will not let you go*" (Deut. 4: 29).

And here for the first time it is taught that man's response to God is to be one of loving (not fearful) obedience. "*Listen, Israel: 'the Eternal, the Eternal alone, is our God.' And you must love the Eternal your God with all your mind and all your soul and all your strength*" (Deut. 6: 4).

It is very striking to find, six hundred years later, that when a young student of the Law asked Jesus, "What is the great commandment in the Law," Jesus drew from him the very words we have just quoted and not, as we might have expected, the more ancient Ten Commandments. That proves that the Book of Deuteronomy had replaced ancient law and had become, with its tremendous social, moral and religious emancipation of the individual, the accepted and authoritative law of the Jewish Church.

But great and beneficial as all these changes most certainly were, the establishment of the new regime could not possibly solve all the problems. The Deuteronomic Reformation carried with it the seeds of its own failure. You can't make people better by "Act of Parliament," even if it is a very spiritually minded "parliament." You cannot, as Francis Thompson taught us fifty years ago, "pack and label souls for God and save them by the barrel-load." The man who pointed that out to Israel in the days when the legislation of Deuteronomy began to take effect was the prophet Jeremiah. In him we have yet another instance of a great truth being born through the mind and experience of a single individual. A great deal of his book is taken up with matters of temporary and local interest and importance and I should not recommend the reader to sit down and read his fifty-two chapters right through. But there are two things which nobody who is studying the Old

Testament ought to miss, because they have a direct bearing upon the responsibilities of the individual and his response to God.

There can be no doubt that Jeremiah must have welcomed the new law whereby everybody went up to worship in the Temple at Jerusalem three times a year, if only because it put an end to the primitive practices and corrupt worship of the local sanctuaries (so bitterly denounced by Amos, Hosea, and Isaiah). But Jeremiah cherished no illusions about this "law of the one sanctuary." He saw what might all too easily come of it. In religion generally and in religious institutions in particular, there is always the danger of confusing means and ends. Elaborate and dignified forms of worship which are intended to be what we call "means of grace," preparing the worshipper for life and helping him to feel beneath the ebb and flow of mundane affairs the thrill and throb of things eternal, may easily become ends in themselves. If that happens, the worshipper may come to take it for granted that having attended public worship he has done something about his religion which is pleasing to God, and very satisfying to himself. Jeremiah had thought clearly and strongly on this matter. He tells us (Ch. 7) how God directed him to go and "stand at the gate of the house of the Lord and deliver this message" to the worshippers as they entered: "*Listen to the Eternal's message, all you who enter by these gates to worship the Eternal . . . Never rely on false phrases like, This is the Eternal's own temple, his very own temple, his very own temple! . . . you are relying on false phrases to no profit.*"

All this may be obvious enough to us. It is to be hoped that we have outgrown the superstition that certain places called temples or churches are more holy than others because God specially dwells in them. But to those who came up to Jerusalem to worship in the Temple it was not so obvious. We know that it is persons who consecrate places, not places persons, but Jeremiah had to remind his contemporaries of this: "*Amend your lives and your doings,*" he says, "*that I (God) may dwell with you in the Temple here.*"

If churchgoing leads individuals to develop by letting worship bring them a new spiritual perspective and more readiness to face moral issues in their own lives, all well and good. But if public worship does not lead to private reformation (what Jeremiah called "amendment of one's doings") then all this attendance at public worship will do more harm than good. It is indeed still possible for religious people to lull their consciences to sleep with stately ritual and soft music and so to live in a fool's paradise, thereby shutting themselves out of the world of reality where they must meet God in the great moral issues which confront their generation.

That brings us to Jeremiah's greatest contribution to the question of the response of man as an individual to the God who, as Amos had taught, "declareth unto man (the individual) what is His thought." Of all Old Testament writers it is Jeremiah who tells us most about himself and his inner life, for here and there in this collection of his writings we seem to be looking over his shoulder as he writes in his private notebook. In his fifteenth chapter he speaks of the terrifying loneliness of his life and complains that he seems to have been born "*to clash and quarrel with the world.*" A deeply sensitive man, he admits to some self-pity. "*Why do I suffer ceaselessly? Why does my wound fester? Am I iron to withstand them? Can my strength hold out?*" He evidently found it a help to write it all down as a kind of prayer, telling God exactly how he felt. But he is equally honest and outspoken in writing what God seemed to say to him by way of answer: "*This,*" he writes, "*was God's answer: 'If you will give up murmuring, I will restore you to my service; if you will purify yourself from passion's dross, then you shall be my spokesman . . . I am with you to succour you'.*" Living in great days for the individual (for that is what the Deuteronomic reformation really meant) Jeremiah had no illusions about human nature: "*Deep is man's mind, deeper than all else on evil bent: who can fathom it?*" But he has no doubts, either, that the man of prayer who goes on his own two feet to God, "*the searcher of the mind and the tester of the heart,*" will be purified of the dross of self-pity or egotism. "*Heal me, O Lord,*" he cries, "*and I shall be healed.*" So finally, in his thirty-first chapter, Jeremiah looks down the long road of experience which seems to open up before the individual who really seeks personal and direct communion with God. He visualises a day, which has

34

not yet dawned upon this earth, when there will be no more need of religious institutions or of those who preside over them and teach in them, because everyone will know God for himself, and will therefore make the full human response to the Divine Will. And he says that this is God's idea of the future of religion. "*A day comes, the Eternal promises, when I will put my law within them, writing it on their hearts, and I will be a God to them and they to me a people; no longer shall they have to teach their fellows, each instructing each how to know God; for they shall all know me, both the great and the small.*" And here is his final word against the old idea of hereditary or communal guilt: "*I will pardon their offences and their sin I will never recall.*"

We can see, then, how true it is that the prophets of the Old Testament prepared the way for the coming of the Christ who, in his own person, fulfilled Jeremiah's great ideal and in so doing opened up the road of that personal religion which is the fulfilment of the destiny of each individual in every age.

CHAPTER FOUR

The Romance of Ruth

DURING both World Wars, many British soldiers married Continental wives. Imagine the heartbreak that would have been caused if the Government had vetoed these marriages and had ordered the wives out of the country, with the grim alternative to the husbands that they themselves would be permanently barred from their native soil if they remained loyal to their wives and accompanied them into banishment. Imagine, too, that this stringent measure to preserve racial purity were condoned and even encouraged by the Church. One's reaction to such an act of despotism would surely be to reflect that in the Royal family itself there flowed a full measure of foreign blood. Yet, astonishing as it may be, this very thing happened in the Jewish nation some three hundred years or so before Christ, under the administrations of Ezra and Nehemiah.

When the tattered remnants of the Israelites returned to their own country after the Babylonian Captivity, many of them were accompanied by the women whom they had married out of foreign tribes. This was against the supreme law of Moses; and in the name of Jehovah, and by the authority of the Mosaic law, Nehemiah set out ruthlessly to destroy all the mixed marriages in the people whom he governed. In his Book, he wrote of the half-Jewish children who could not even speak the Jewish language but chattered amongst themselves in the dialect of Ashdod. He continues, "And I contended with . . . the Jews that had married women of Ashdod, of Ammon and of Moab . . . and cursed them, and smote certain of them, and plucked off their hair, and made them swear by God that they would not marry their daughters to the sons of foreigners, nor marry their sons to their daughters, nor marry foreigners themselves. 'Was not this the sin of Solomon king of Israel? There was no king like him in all the nations; yet even he was led into sin by his foreign wives. And is it to be thought of that you should do this great evil and break faith with our God by marrying foreign wives?' "

Nehemiah's predecessor, Ezra, had behaved in a slightly more humane fashion by plucking off his own hair and beard instead of other people's. Even so, he made an end of over a hundred of these marriages, and put on record a list of one hundred and thirteen families that were broken up at his instigation. It is easy to imagine the heartrending scenes that must have taken place as this fanatical priest went about his merciless mission.

Ezra does not record how many Jews remained faithful to their foreign wives and left the country: but rather than endure so tragic a break-up of their family life, many men must have taken the hard decision to face permanent exile from their native land. Indeed, these inhuman acts carried out in the name of God set people thinking and murmuring; and one person, who wisely remained anonymous, hit upon an idea for confronting the authorities with a subtle argument against their rigorous policy. He set it down in the most readable form of a story of the days of old, in the time "when the Judges ruled Israel," and gave it to the people and to posterity in the form of the Book of Ruth.

In our Bible, this book follows the Book of Judges; and so gentle and pastoral a story may at first sight appear out of place and in sharp contrast with the bloodthirsty narratives that precede it. But in the Hebrew Bible, the Book of Ruth appears among the five "Festal Rolls" (of which the others are The Song of Songs, Lamentations, Ecclesiastes and Esther). This grouping itself suggests that the book is of late date and does not belong to the far-off period of the Judges. The compilers of the Greek Old Testament, however, doubtless gave it its position as we have it today because of its opening words, "In the days when the Judges ruled." But that the book was written some hundreds of years after the time of the Judges is authenticated by the occurrence in the script of words in Aramaic—a language that did not come into popular use until some time after the return from the Exile in Babylon.

It is only four chapters long, but beautifully narrated. Indeed, Goethe, the great German writer, pronounced it to be "the loveliest little idyll that tradition has handed down to us." For sheer literary beauty, read it as it stands in the Authorised Version, but Dr. James Moffatt will give you the best interpretation of some of the more archaic phrases used in the Authorised Version.

The story, briefly, is this:

In the time of the Judges—that dark age when every man's hand was against his brother, and many a woman disgraced her sex as shamefully as Jael or Delilah—there was a famine in the land of Israel, and a family from Bethlehem-Judah went and settled in the land of Moab. They had not been there long when Elimelech, the father, died and his wife, Naomi, was left with her two sons. They both married Moabite girls, one named Orpah and other Ruth. Ten years later, the sons also died: and now Naomi, hearing that food was again plentiful in Israel, set out on the road for her old home. But the bond between her and her two daughters-in-law was very strong and they both begged to go with her. Naomi tried to dissuade them, saying, "Go, return each to her mother's house: the Lord deal kindly with you as ye have dealt with the dead and with me. The Lord grant you that ye may find rest each of you in the house of her husband. . . . Turn again, my daughters; why will ye go with me?" They persisted, with tears, until finally Orpah was persuaded and kissed her mother-in-law goodbye. Ruth, however, clung to Naomi.

For the last time, Naomi said, *"Behold, thy sister-in-law is gone back to her people and her God: return thou after thy sister-in-law."* But Ruth would not leave her. *"Intreat me not to leave thee and to return from following thee,"* she said, *"for whither thou goest I will go, and where thou lodgest I will lodge: thy people shall be my people, and thy God my God: where thou diest will I die and there will I be buried. The Lord do so to me and more also, if aught but death part thee and me."* So Naomi and Ruth came to the old home; and their arrival set the whole town astir.

Now one of the chief men of the town was Boaz, a kinsman of Elimelech, the late husband of Naomi. As it was the beginning of the barley harvest, Ruth offered to go gleaning; and by chance she entered one of Boaz' fields. Her reputation for faithfulness to the family had preceded her, and Boaz singled her out and praised her for the care she had taken of her mother-in-law. He invited her to share the reapers' meal, and ordered his men to show her proper respect. On reaching home that evening, Ruth told her mother-in-law how kindly this man Boaz had treated her; whereupon Naomi, delighted, explained who he was. Ruth gleaned every day in Boaz' field, until both the barley and the wheat harvests were over and it was time for threshing.

Wishing to see Ruth settled, Naomi advised her to claim the kinship of Boaz, who would then have the right to purchase the land that had belonged to Elimelech. (By custom, he would also assume responsibility for the widow of his late kinsman's son, and in marrying her, perpetuate the family name.) Following Naomi's instructions, Ruth crept unseen into the threshing-floor where, having supervised the day's work, Boaz lay asleep by the heap of grain. When he awoke, and found her there, she claimed his protection: but while he welcomed her, he also explained that there was a nearer kinsman who had prior rights to his. He then sent her home with a present of grain for her mother-in-law, whilst he himself took the necessary steps to enquire of this near kinsman whether or not he wished to claim his rights. The kins-man at first agreed to do so. But when Boaz pointed out that if he bought the piece of land that had belonged to Elimelech, he would also be expected to marry Ruth the Moabitess, and carry on the name of the dead along with his inheritance, he said he could not, "for fear of injuring his own inheritance." So in the presence of ten elders of the town, he relinquished his rights and, in accordance with ancient custom, drew off his shoe, giving it to Boaz, "for this was," the writer explains, "the form of attestation in Israel." At the Town Gate, where all public and private affairs were carried out, Boaz called on ten of the Sheikhs to act as wit-nesses to the transaction. This they did, and together with all the rest of the people there, they invoked the blessing of God upon Boaz and Ruth. In this way, Ruth found her second Jewish husband. Let the author tell the rest of the story in his own words: "So Boaz took Ruth, and she became his wife: and when he went in unto her, the Lord gave her conception, and she bare a son. And the women said to Naomi, 'Blessed be the Lord, which hath not left thee this day without a near kinsman, and may his name

4

be famous in Israel. And he shall be unto thee a restorer of thy life, and a nourisher of thy old age: for thy daughter-in-law, which loveth thee, which is better to thee than seven sons, hath borne him.' And Naomi took the child, and laid it in her bosom, and became nurse unto it. And the women her neighbours gave it a name, saying, 'There is a son born to Naomi'; and they called his name Obed: he is the father of Jesse, the father of David."

Read the Book of Ruth keeping in mind the background of the period of national reconstruction against which it was written, and it becomes clear that this historical romance was a protest against the cruel marriage laws enforced so rigorously in the author's own day, and contained a passionate appeal to inhuman nationalism to stay its hand. Read again Ruth's loving appeal to Naomi: "Intreat me not to leave thee and to return from following after thee: for whither thou goest I will go, and where thou lodgest I will lodge: thy people shall be my people, and thy God my God: where thou diest I will die and there will I be buried. The Lord do so to me, and more also, if aught but death part thee and me." Can one not hear in that the pleading of those hundred and thirteen foreign wives, and many more, with their Jewish husbands, when the Commissioners of Ezra and Nehemiah served them with notice to quit by the first day of the next month? And was not the appeal of the book of Ruth even more poignant in that it was made through the faithfulness of this foreign widow to her Jewish mother-in-law and not simply to her Jewish husband? But the writer evidently knew full well the awful power of nationalist pride, especially when it is wedded to religious authority. So he kept his trump card up his sleeve till the end, indeed to the very last word of his book. And that word is "David." "Have you forgotten," he seems to be saying, "that the great King, the man after God's own heart, the founder of your national greatness, the sweet singer of Israel, had foreign blood in his veins, for he was the great-grandson of Ruth the Moabitess? Supposing there had been a law in those days to prevent Boaz from marrying Ruth, you might never have had the Davidic Dynasty!"

Whether or not the Book of Ruth had any success as an effective liberal protest against inhuman marriage laws in the author's own time, it is certainly entitled to its place in Biblical literature. Protests, especially religious protests, are so often as negative as the evils against which they are made; but this book will stand for ever as a model of constructive criticism. Read in this light, the Book of Ruth has considerable spiritual relevance to some of those controversies of our own time which arise from race prejudice and all forms of rigorist legislation, whether civil or ecclesiastical. Institutions, even Churches, can become very inhuman and often tend to sacrifice natural human relationships to policies of expediency. We are for ever indebted to this anonymous liberal of an illiberal age for keeping alive through his story of Ruth the Moabitess a divine discontent with the *status quo*. *"Where the spirit of the Lord is, there is liberty,"* wrote the great Apostle of the Gentiles. Never was there a greater need for that spirit than in our day, when the tide of totalitarianism is steadily encroaching upon the rights and liberties of the individual, who, according to the teaching of the Bible, Old and New Testaments alike, has been placed in this world to develop his or her personality through human relationships into the glorious liberty of the children of God.

CHAPTER FIVE

The Patience of Job

"IF I knew of a boss who let his business get into anything like the mess that God has allowed the world to get into today, I'd get him sacked!" The businessman who said that, during a fireside discussion in which I was taking part, was not saying anything new. He was only repeating in his own way the complaint of thousands of thinking people of every generation. James Russell Lowell gave classic expression to it years ago: "If about to make such another world as this, O God, stay thine hand."

It is the weighty and unsolved problem of Pain that constitutes the greatest obstacle to faith. Earthquakes, volcanic eruptions, floods and avalanches periodically take their toll of human life and human endeavour. Even today, there are seven hundred million sufferers from malaria alone, and in India more than twenty thousand people die of snakebite in one year and about three thousand are destroyed by wild beasts. And leaving aside such things as are largely outside human control, there is that great burden of pain and tragedy which is entirely the consequence of man's inhumanity to man.

But as the discussion proceeded I found that it was not this large general question of suffering which was troubling my friend. He was quite prepared to admit that all these natural disasters must be accepted in the light of the facts revealed by modern science that we live in a universe and a world in the making and must therefore put up with the consequent inconveniences, which should be thought of as being part of the Creator's unsolved problems or, in some cases, attributable to the misuse of human free will. What was really troubling him was a more strictly personal matter. He had recently had more than his share of misfortune, and he was smarting under a sense of injustice—Why should all this have happened to him, and what had he done to deserve it?

Now, no purely intellectual explanation of this difficulty is of much use, because the problem involves a man's whole personality

—his feelings and his spirit as well as his mind. All that we can do is to try and find the right attitude to take towards it. It is perilously easy to drift into a negative attitude and to become embittered and cynical: it is much harder to stiffen the upper lip and, with R. L. Stevenson, to go on believing in the ultimate decency of things "even if one awakes in hell." It was to encourage people to adopt this positive attitude of acceptance of one's personal share of misfortune and suffering that an unknown author wrote the Book of Job.

In the days before we had examined the Old Testament critically, it used to be thought that the Book of Job was one of the oldest among the books of the Bible, but today we can see, not only by its style but also by the ideas of God contained in its poetry, that it belongs to as late a period as that of the second Isaiah (Ch. 40 onwards), probably about the close of the sixth century B.C. But there is something else which points to this late date in Israel's story. We have seen (Ch. 3) that it was not until after the teaching of the great prophets, especially Jeremiah, that the problem of the suffering of the individual man or woman could possibly arise. It would never have occurred to the mind of a writer in the earlier days to raise the question which is in the forefront of the mind of the author of "Job," "What is the meaning of suffering?"—and still less, "Why do good people suffer?" According to the teaching of those early days, if evil of any kind overtook you and you suffered, it would be said that God had been offended in some way by what your forefathers or your fellow tribesmen had done. Their sins were believed to be visited upon their children "unto the third and fourth generation." All that could be done was for the priestly oracle to prescribe a sacrifice to put things right. It would never have occurred to anyone to protest against the punishment of innocent people, if it was believed that the tribe had sinned; their punishment, usually by death, was necessary for reasons of national security, as we should say. But when, as we have seen, the prophets tried to demolish those barbarous notions and began to teach the personal importance and personal responsibilities of the individual, and that God really does deal with us one by one and not in the mass, a totally different

43

answer had to be found to the question, "Why do men suffer?"
The prophets Jeremiah and Ezekiel had to be content to stress the
responsibility of the individual for his own life and his own sins.
In their own way of putting it they said, "*Ye shall no more say, the
fathers have eaten sour grapes and the children's teeth are set on edge*"—
that is to say, "you are not suffering for the sins of past generations;
you are suffering because of your own misdoings." And Ezekiel
went further and said, "*The soul that sinneth, it shall die*," by which
of course he did not mean that everyone who sins will be punished
by death, but that if you do suffer and die, it will be for your *own*
sins and not for those of your great grandfather or your fellow
tribesmen. Upon that broad general teaching, which was
obviously a great improvement on what had gone before, smaller
minds soon got to work.

People with literal minds will always debase the teaching of the
great spiritual leaders by trying to reduce it to a sort of rule of
thumb affair. That is the kind of thing that happened over the
problems raised by human suffering. It came to be believed and
taught that every ache and pain that you get, whether in the body
or the mind, is God's direct punishment for one or other of your
sins. In short, "so much sin, so much suffering." God was thought
of as a sort of celestial (or infernal!) dispenser who put your sins
in one scale and an equivalent amount of toothache, jaundice or
rheumatism in the other, and that is what you got. And it was
taught that you must, in spite of everything, cling to your belief
in God's sense of justice to make the punishment fit the crime.
How such a view managed to gain acceptance and to hold the
field for hundreds of years, and how the last remaining vestiges
of it still survive into the twentieth century (and they do!) almost
passes comprehension. But so it was and so, to a large extent, it
still is. Do you doubt that it is still at the back of people's minds?
A hospital chaplain could remove all doubt. Half a dozen times a
week he will be asked, "What have I done to deserve this?" or,
"Why should this happen to me?"; and then almost invariably
the patient will add that, after all, he's no worse than anybody else.
Clearly, the connection between personal sin and personal
suffering is still very much in people's minds.

Now that is precisely the view which the author of the Book of Job wished to challenge, for we know that it was always taken for granted in those days that if you suffered you must have sinned and that your sufferings were God's direct punishment for your sins. So this author takes the case of an exceptionally righteous and upright individual, whom he calls Job, and then proceeds to plague him with all the ills that flesh is heir to, within a week. That is his first major point. Job is described as "*perfect and upright, and one that feared God and eschewed evil.*" He is also exceedingly prosperous and is described as "*the greatest of the sons of the east.*" (Prosperity, you must know, was regarded as a sure sign of the Divine favour.) Within a few days Job loses everything. His flocks and herds are either stolen by bandits or struck by lightning, his seven sons and three daughters, feasting in their eldest brother's house, are crushed to death under their own roof which is blown in on them by a great wind from the desert; and finally Job himself is smitten with sore boils from top to toe. But amidst this avalanche of disaster which has reduced him to utter misery, the patient man, even in spite of the taunts of his wife, "holds fast by his integrity" and denies that he has sinned. "*What?*" he says, "*Shall we receive good at the hand of God, and shall we not receive evil? . . . Naked came I forth from my mother's womb, and naked shall I return: the Lord gave and the Lord hath taken away—Blessed be the name of the Lord!*" Job is indeed a wonderful example of the man who can "take it."

All this is described in the highly dramatic prologue which occupies the first two chapters. But this prologue contains something more. The author, making full use of ancient Jewish mythology, keeps changing the scene from earth, where all these disasters keep piling up, to the celestial regions where they are supposed to have been carefully and maliciously arranged by "The Adversary," who is called "Satan" (not to be confused with "The Devil" of later belief). This "Satan" or Adversary, whom we might perhaps call the personification of the spite of circumstances, is portrayed as "presenting himself before the Lord" with all the other angels and reporting on the conduct of men. He suggests that Job, who is the apple of God's eye, is only good because he finds that it pays. *"Skin for skin,"* he says, *"Put forth thine hand now, and touch all that he hath, and he will curse thee to thy face."* God is pictured as accepting the challenge. *"Behold,"* he replies, *"he is in thine hand: only, spare his life."* By this ingenious dramatic device, our author was trying to make a distinction (which always must be made) between what God wills and what God allows, and so provided perplexed minds with what we should regard as a sort of interim solution which was that suffering should be accepted as "a godly discipline" instead of a punishment. But don't forget that this is nothing more than an interim solution.

That leads us on to the main part of the book, which takes the form of a discussion between Job and his three friends, Eliphaz, Bildad and Zophar. These three friends have rightly earned their unenviable though entirely justifiable title of "Job's comforters." They all three take much the same line with him, which could be briefly summarised as follows:

"You have always appeared to everybody to have justified your reputation as an exemplary father and citizen; but now that all this has come upon you it is obvious that you must have been as great a sinner as the rest of us, for 'who ever perished, being innocent?' You must therefore accept your sufferings as 'the chastening of the Almighty' and amend your life." Cold comfort indeed!

The three friends monotonously reiterate their arguments and Job always gives them the same answer, stoutly maintaining that he is not conscious of any misconduct that could possibly justify God in punishing him. In Chapter 12, after a particularly provocative speech of Zophar's, Job comes near to losing his temper, and delivers himself of the magnificent and now famous retort which begins:

"No doubt but ye are the people, and wisdom shall die with you. But I have understanding as well as you; I am not inferior to you . . ."

and continues:

"Ye are forgers of lies, ye are all physicians of no value. O that ye would altogether hold your peace!"

and ends with the dignified reminder that after all none of us live long enough to be dogmatic in these great matters.

> "*Man that is born of a woman is of few days,*
>   *And full of trouble.*
> *He cometh forth like a flower, and is cut down:*
> *He fleeth also as a shadow, and continueth not.*"

But this is not enough to silence the pious platitudes of his friends, who have already more than earned their classic title. Even when Job utters his noblest protest—"*Though He slay me, yet will I trust in Him*" (Ch. 13 : 15)—they still persist in taxing him with sinfulness.

> "*Is not thy wickedness great? And thine iniquities infinite?*
> *Acquaint now thyself with God, and be at peace:*
> *Thereby good shall come to thee*" (Ch. 22: 21).

But how is one to acquaint oneself with God? Here the author introduces his master-stroke.

The God who had "called" Abraham and had spoken to Moses "face to face, as a man speaketh with his friend," now speaks to his suffering servant, Job. God takes the initiative. Man has now had his say, and all that he has said about the dark enigma of suffering is futile and unconvincing. The things that Job's three friends have said about God are simply not true (42:7). Therefore God Himself must now have the last word.

> "*Then the Lord answered Job out of the whirlwind, and said, Who is this that darkeneth counsel by words without knowledge?*"

The "Voice of Deity" occupies the rest of the book, and it should be read at a sitting because it is really the author's final answer to Job's problem. It does not offer an explanation of suffering but it suggests an attitude. Thomas Carlyle gave much the same answer in the language of our own time, when he wrote, "To the minnow, every cranny and pebble and accident of its little native creek may have become familiar; but does the minnow

understand the ocean tides and periodic currents, the trade-winds
and monsoons and moon's eclipses, by all which this condition of
its little creek is regulated, and may from time to time be overset
and reversed? Such a minnow is Man; his creek this planet Earth;
his ocean the immeasurable All; his monsoons and periodic
currents the mysterious course of Providence through aeons of
aeons."

So through the majestic vision of the forces of Nature, God
challenges the querulous complaints of Man against His inscru-
table ordering of the world (Ch. 38). Chapter 39 continues the
survey in which, through a series of more detailed pictures of the
wonder and beauty of animal life, the sufferer's eyes are opened to
the workmanship of God. The finest of these is perhaps the
description of the war-horse.

"Hast thou given the horse his might?
Hast thou clothed his neck with the quivering mane?
Hast thou made him to leap like a locust?
The glory of his snorting is terrible.
He paweth in the valley, and rejoiceth in his strength:
He goeth forth to meet the armed men.
He mocketh at fear, and is not dismayed;
Neither turneth he back from the sword.
The quiver rattleth against him,
The flashing spear and the javelin.
He swalloweth the ground with fierceness and rage;
Neither standeth he still at the voice of the trumpet.
As oft as the trumpet soundeth, he saith Aha!
He smelleth the battle afar off,
The thunder of the captains, and the shouting."

Then at last (Ch. 42) comes the final confession of Job. He has
been lifted out of himself and his misery by the overwhelming
splendour of God's creation. There is, he is able now to say,
wisdom in all things, even in the things which he cannot understand; a wisdom too great for mortal man to question.

Moffatt's translation gives a more accurate rendering of Job's
reply than the Authorised Version.

"I am of small account: how can I answer thee?
I lay my hand upon my lips;
Once I have spoken—never again!
Twice—but I will not say one other word!
I admit thou canst do anything,
That nothing is too hard for thee.
I thoughtlessly confused the issues;
I spoke without intelligence
    Of wonders far beyond my ken.
I had heard of thee by hearsay,
    But now mine eyes have seen thee;
So I despise myself,
In dust and ashes I repent."

One cannot but feel that this was the end of the original work. What follows (Ch. 42: 7–17) is not on anything like the same high level of inspiration. Indeed it is in the nature of an anti-climax. Job is said to have been restored to his former prosperity "and more than at the beginning." Fourteen thousand sheep now instead of his original seven thousand, double the number of his camels, and another family of seven sons and three daughters as at first.

Is not this the work of a later editor who wished to preserve the orthodox notion that prosperity is a sign of the Divine favour—the very idea which the original author was at pains to destroy? The author of the New Testament Epistle of James, however, evidently approved of it, for after exhorting his readers to imitate the patience of Job, he mentions "the end of God's way" with him as an instance of the divine compassion. I would prefer to think that the original author wished to teach through his great dramatic poem that the patience which was born in Job through his suffering was his all sufficient reward. A man who has come to the nobility of Job does not need compassion or compensation. He comes forth like gold tried in the fire, not ennobled by suffering—for suffering never ennobled anyone—but ennobled by the attitude God has enabled him to take towards it. Perhaps out English poet T. E. Brown had Job in mind when he wrote in his poem, "Pain,"

49

"The man that hath great griefs I pity not;
'Tis something to be great
In any wise, and hint the larger state.

. . . .

To him the sorrows are the tension thrills
    Of that serene endeavour,
Which yields to God for ever and for ever
The joy that is more ancient than the hills."

NOTE TO CHAPTER FIVE

THE Book of Job is the nearest thing in the Bible to what we should call a problem play. This is disguised from the ordinary reader by the way it is printed in the Authorised Version. (The Revised Version is a little better because it has substituted the paragraph for the verse division. But even then it is difficult to read the book as a drama.) So I transcribe here the Title Page as it would appear if the book were published today. (I owe this to R. G. Moulton's *Modern Reader's Bible*, an invaluable volume containing the text of scripture in its proper literary forms.)

THE BOOK OF JOB

A dramatic Poem framed in an Epic Story.

Persons of the Story
The Lord.
The Sons of God, or Guardian Spirits.
The Adversary: Guardian Spirit of the Earth.
Job.
The Wife of Job.
The Friends of Job.
Messengers.

The scene of the story changes between Heaven and the House of Job in the land of Uz.

The Patience of Job

Persons of the Drama

Job.
Eliphaz the Temanite ⎫
Bildad the Shuhite ⎬ Friends of Job.
Zophar the Naamathite ⎭
Elihu the Buzite, a young man.
Spectators (mute).
Voice out of the Whirlwind.

Scene of the Drama: The ash-mound outside a village in the Land of Uz.

CHAPTER SIX

The Adventure of Jonah

A BOOK was published some years ago which bore the title, *God is my Adventure*. Many a Biblical author, especially the great prophets Jeremiah and Ezekiel, might quite justifiably have published some of their writings under a similar title. Some of their descriptions of situations into which they were led as the result of following what had been disclosed to them as the will of God are so graphic as to appear fantastic and grotesque if we take them literally.

Every teacher and preacher knows how difficult it is to get truth across, especially to an illiterate audience, and these prophets of the Old Testament seem to have found it necessary at times to put on a kind of charade or dumb-show to attract attention and to convey a message. Ezekiel, for example, wishing to warn the heedless citizens of Jerusalem of an impending siege, was instructed to take a brick, place it in front of him, trace upon it a plan of Jerusalem and then "lay siege to it." After that he was to lie for a hundred and ninety days on his left side and forty days on his right side to betoken the years of captivity in store for Israel and Judah respectively. How far this is a description of what the prophet actually did, or how far it may be his highly dramatic way of recording his message, it is impossible to tell. When, however, he describes other experiences of his like the famous vision of the Valley of the Dry Bones (Ch. 37), he is careful to tell us that the whole experience took place when "the hand of God was upon him," and that he was "carried away in the Spirit." In other places he says that he was "in a trance." After the extremely graphic description of his experience by the River of Chebar (Ch. 1), he says, "Such was the *appearance* of what *resembled* the splendour of the Lord."

Once it is recognised that these Biblical writers made as full use of symbolism and allegory as a writer like Hans Andersen, all the difficulties which were felt at one time about the book of Jonah vanish at a touch.

There is certainly no book in the whole Bible which has been an easier target for the mockery of its enemies or a greater embarrassment to those who wish to uphold its truth than the Book of Jonah. And of course both the mockery and the embarrassment have arisen from the whale—or more accurately the "great fish"—which is said to have swallowed the prophet and then at the divine command to have obediently regurgitated him "upon the dry land."

In one of his "Palace plays" called *Religious Difficulties*, Mr. Laurence Housman has depicted Queen Victoria discussing the matter with the Dean of Windsor. The Queen imperiously demands a plain answer to a plain question. "Did God provide a great fish capable of swallowing Jonah, or did he not?" The Dean at first moves obliquely (like a Bishop in chess) and suggests that of course God *could* have done so if He had wished; but, when pressed, affirms that in his opinion "upon the whole, He did not" —an opinion with which the good Queen and most of us would entirely agree. But of course neither the difficulty nor the mockery would have ever arisen about this whale had not this brilliant psychological study by an unknown writer of the third or fourth century B.C. become Scripture. Seldom has an author with a great message to his contemporaries been so completely victimised by the literal minded and the unimaginative. The trouble has all arisen because of the theory (still defended by some) that we must "take the Bible literally."

Once we have disposed of the necessity for a literal interpretation, the difficulties vanish and we shall be able to arrive at the real meaning of the book which, as I have already said, is a psychological study of the religious consciousness of Israel after the return from the Exile in Babylon. From a considerable amount of evidence, especially in the books of Ezra and Nehemiah, we can feel at once the thrill and the tension of these repatriated exiles. We are told that "they sang one to another in praising and giving thanks unto the Lord, saying, for he is good, for his mercy endureth for ever towards Israel" (Ezra 3: 11). But when some of their neighbours came forward with an offer of help in re-building the Temple, the Jews would have nothing to do with them. *"Let us build with you,"* they pleaded, *"for we seek your God, as ye do"; but the heads of fathers' houses in Israel said unto them, "Ye have nothing to do with us to build an house unto our God; but we ourselves together will build unto the Lord, the God of Israel"* (Ezra 4: 3). In our study of the Book of Ruth we saw the same exclusive nationalism at work in regard to marriage with non-Jews. In short, the attitude of the returned exiles towards all foreigners was that reflected by the last lines of Psalm 137:

> "O Daughter of Babylon, who art to be destroyed;
> Blessed shall he be that rewardeth thee as thou hast
> served us.
> Blessed shall he be that taketh and dasheth thy little ones
> against the stones."

That started the feud with the Samaritans which lasted right on till the days of Christ, four hundred years later, when we are told that "Jews have no dealings with Samaritans," whom they regarded and spoke of as Gentile dogs, "lesser breeds without the law."

Now it was into that atmosphere of nationalist exclusiveness and spiritual snobbishness that the anonymous author of the book of Jonah projected his message. He evidently belonged, like the author of the book of Ruth, to a more liberal school of thought. Just as the author of "Ruth" had pointed out the inhumanity of the government's attitude to foreign marriages, so the author of "Jonah" wished to protest against the intolerant attitude of the Jewish Church and even of some who called themselves God's spokesmen (prophets) towards the whole heathen world. So to our story:

It is significant that the author chose as his subject "Jonah the son of Amittai." He was an historical character referred to in II Kings 14 as having encouraged the imperialistic ambitions of the King (Jeroboam II) and he is designated as a "prophet" ("the prophet which was of Gathhepher"). But he had lived a good three hundred years before the time of our author—that is to say, long before "Nineveh" had come into the picture. It is therefore clear that the writer is only using Jonah's name to represent the extreme nationalist school of thought which regarded all non-Jews as outside the pale. So the little Book of Jonah is not a history but an allegory. That justifies us in reading Nationalist Israel, in its hard-hearted exclusiveness, for Jonah; the whole heathen (non-Jewish) world for Nineveh; and Babylon for the "great fish", which had literally swallowed the Hebrew people and then "vomited" them again in sending the exiles home.

Jonah receives a message from God to go and preach to the Ninevites. He immediately books his passage on a ship "going to Tarshish" (that is, a ship going in exactly the opposite direction, "to flee unto Tarshish from the presence of the Lord"), which means that from the start Jonah resists his call to missionary enterprise. The author repeats this phrase *"fleeing from the presence of the Lord"* three times, as if to say, "D'you see how obstinately this so-called prophet tried to run away from God?" It also rather interestingly reflects the primitive belief (so frequently found in the earlier parts of the Old Testament) that God was subject to the limitations of geography, so that by changing your location to non-Jewish soil you got outside his jurisdiction. (The story of Naaman the Syrian taking two mules' burdens of Israelite soil home with him is a good instance of the same belief (II Kings 5 : 17). But Jonah finds that he cannot evade God by getting on to the high seas, so, when a terriffc storm sweeps down upon the ship, instead of lending a hand to the terrified sailors, he goes below with his burdened conscience. He is not even as religious or as practical as these heathen sailors who in their peril cry "every man unto his god" and lighten the ship of her cargo. He just sleeps through it, until the captain comes up to him and says, *"What meanest thou, O Sleeper? Arise, call upon thy God, if so be that God will think upon us that we perish not."* The mention of God, and that by a heathen shipmaster, is too much for Jonah and he unburdens his tortured mind to the ship's company. He tells them the awful truth that he is running away from God and that the storm is on his account and that all he can suggest is that he, Jonah, shall be thrown overboard. *"Take me up,"* he says, *"and cast me forth into the sea; so shall the sea be calm unto you: for I know that for my sake this great tempest is upon you."* Here again one feels that the author is pouring scorn on the primitive idea that "Sheol" (the place of departed spirits) was beyond the reach of God (*"for in death no man remembereth thee, and who shall give thee thanks in the pit?"*). Jonah hopes that death will deliver him from all further contact with God, whose direct orders he has disobeyed. But once more he is disappointed. *"And the Lord prepared a great fish to swallow up Jonah; and Jonah was in the belly of the fish three days and three nights."*

Chapter 2 is a poem which obviously cannot have belonged to the original book, as it is a thanksgiving for deliverance from the perils of the sea. It is totally inappropriate in this place, for Jonah's mood was anything but one of thanksgiving. He did not wish to be rescued from the perils of the sea or any other perils except that of the *"presence of the Lord."* It might have been more appropriate after 2:10, when the great fish has *"vomited him out on dry land,"* but even then the whole thing is out of character. It must have been interpolated by a later editor who wished to moralise and to *improve* the occasion.

That brings us to the original author's close psychological study of his country's flinty-hearted and superior attitude towards the heathen world through the behaviour of Jonah after he has been landed, very much against his will, within striking distance of Nineveh. Indeed, Jonah finds himself, in one day's journey, in the heart of the great city. Here he delivers his message of doom: *"Yet forty days and Nineveh shall be overthrown."* The Prophet's word takes immediate effect. From the King, who immediately proclaims a fast, down to the very beasts, everybody is covered with sackcloth and ashes, with the result that *"God saw their works, that they turned from their evil ways, and God repented him of the evil which he had said he would do unto them, and he did it not."*

Few prophets could have claimed a more complete success for their preaching, and most prophets would have been humbly thankful for it. But not Jonah! *"It displeased Jonah exceedingly, and he was angry."* In the bitterness of his soul he prays for death. *"O Lord, take, I beseech thee, my life from me; for it is better for me to die than to live."* He feels that God has let him down and shown most unreasonable clemency and mercy to these wretched heathen. He had come there simply to proclaim the city's doom, and now he feels that God has made a fool of him by reversing the sentence. He goes out into the eastern suburbs and builds a little hut for himself, and sits *"under it in the shadow, till he might see what would become of the city."* In a word, Jonah spends the rest of the day in a sulk, still rather hoping that perhaps the city will after all be destroyed. That reveals a still more serious disease in the prophet's soul. It is not just wounded pride in having been made to look ridiculous; it is a terrible, ruthless, unrelenting hatred that he has of these heathen people. That is revealed by the author, who puts into his mouth the bitterest words of all.

"Was not this my saying when I was yet in my own country? . . . for I knew that thou art a gracious God and full of compassion, slow to anger, and of great kindness, and repentest thee of the evil."

In plain English, Jonah takes it upon himself to tell God exactly what he thinks of him! He is not at all a God after Jonah's own fanatical heart, because he is far too merciful and compassionate towards the heathen. Here is the peak point of Jonah's complaint. In his estimation, God ought to be as great a rigorist as himself and his fellow countrymen. He is in the same frame of mind as some of the Psalmists who expressed themselves still more forcibly in some of the "cursing" psalms.

"Pour out thine indignation upon the heathen that have not known thee: and upon the kingdoms that have not called upon thy name" (79: 6).

"Consume them in wrath, consume them, that they may not be: and let them know that God ruleth in Jacob unto the ends of the earth" (59: 13).

It is a sad fact, and greatly to the discredit of the Christian Church, that owing to the view of the infallibility of Scripture, these "cursing" psalms are still sometimes used in Christian worship. As specimens of the lengths to which spiritual pride and fanatical nationalism can carry men, they are valuable memorials; but to permit their use by a Christian congregation in the worship of the

God and Father of Jesus Christ is nothing short of blasphemy. It could well be said of them what Erasmus said of the battle standards which he saw adorning our Churches, that they are "bloodstained memorials of human depravity."

But to return to Jonah. We are next shown how God proceeded to deal with his rebellious prophet. If he had been the kind of God Jonah thought He ought to be, He would have struck him dead on the spot, and Jonah seems to have continued to wish that He would. But instead God patiently proceeds with the man's spiritual education. Nineveh is a great city containing more than a hundred and twenty thousand inhabitants who *"know not their right hand from their left."* But for all their numbers, God has a concern for each individual soul amongst them, foolish and ignorant as they are. That is the next lesson that Jonah has to learn. As he sat there sulking outside the city, *"the sun beat upon the head of Jonah, that he fainted,"* so God provided him with kindly shelter. *"The Lord God prepared a gourd, and made it to come up over Jonah, that it might be a shadow over his head, to deliver him from his grief."* For this the prophet was grateful: *"he was exceeding glad because of the gourd."* This was, of course, to teach him that God still goes on caring even for people as foolish and ignorant as he. But evidently this was not enough to soften Jonah's heart for the Ninevites, whom he still thought to be much more ignorant and worthless than himself. Therefore God had to try another expedient. *"God prepared a worm when the morning rose the next day, and it smote the gourd that it withered."* That is a very subtle touch! By introducing the worm to consume the gourd and closely following up this destruction of his shelter by a parching wind and a scorching sun, the author is suggesting that God permitted Jonah to think for a little while that the Deity was *"even such an one as himself,"* that is, a destructive, cruel God. The immediate result is a still more bitter outburst of anger from the prophet. *"It is better for me to die than to live."* So at last God gets Jonah where he wants him, so to speak, and makes him angry with his own false thoughts of God. *"And God said to Jonah, Doest thou well to be angry for the gourd? And he said, I do well to be angry, even unto death."*

It looks as if this must be the end and that nothing will avail to change Jonah's idea of God. But it is not. God's patience abides man's inhumanity to man, and into the stony heart of Jonah there creeps one tiny grain of compassion. God detects it and immediately calls the prophet's attention to it: "*Thou hast had pity on the gourd.*" It is as if God were telling him that He is glad to find that the milk of human kindness has not quite dried up in him. "*Thou hast had pity on the gourd, for the which thou hast not laboured, neither madest it grow; which came up in a night, and perished in a night: And should not I spare Nineveh, that great city, wherein are more than six-score thousand persons that cannot discern between their right hand and their left hand?*"

So the message of the great prophets, from Isaiah to Ezekiel, of the importance of the individual in God's sight, is once again driven home. God does not deal with the children of men as tribes or nations or "the masses," but as individuals like Jonah, one by one. And this brilliant author goes even further and teaches that the Creator has a concern not only for men and women but even for the animal world as well, for he adds "*and much cattle.*" Those are actually the last words of the book.

If we were to try and read Jonah as our ancestors did, as a story of actual fact, the whole thing would be unworthy of its place in the Scriptures. But taken as an allegory, it is one of the greatest treasures of the Old Testament. Its anonymous author stands on the same high level of inspiration as the Second Isaiah who flung out precisely the same challenge to the repatriated Jewish exiles.

> " '*Tis too slight a service to set the clans of Jacob up again, and restore Israel's survivors;*
> *I now appoint you to bring light to the nations, that my salvation may reach the world's end.*"

So the adventure of Jonah is well placed near the end of the Old Testament, for the writer's emphasis on "the tender mercy of our God" towards the whole human race brings him in spirit very near to Christ. According to him, as according to Christ, God is for ever seeking Man much more unceasingly and passionately than Man is seeking God. The God of Jonah is, as Francis Thompson called Him, "The Hound of Heaven," the Love that will not let us go, Who, when at last He overtakes us as we run from Him in our folly and blindness, cries,

> "Ah, fondest, blindest, weakest,
> I am He whom thou seekest!
> Thou dravest love from thee, who dravest Me."

CHAPTER SEVEN

The Manna of the Church

JUST over three hundred years ago Dr. John Donne, one of the most famous of the Deans of St. Paul's, described the Book of Psalms as "the Manna of the Church." Manna, as the reader of Exodus will recall, was the food—probably coriander seed (Exod. 17: 31)—which the wandering tribes of Israel gathered in the dew of the morning. It is said to have "tasted like wafers made with honey." According to the ancient writer, although it became their regular diet they were not allowed to store it up but were told to gather it fresh every morning. So the great preacher's suggestion is that in order to get the best out of the Psalms we should always turn to them with a fresh mind as though we had never read them before.

It was a great deal easier for a seventeenth century audience to do that than it is for us, because they were the first generation of Englishmen to read the Psalms (or indeed any considerable parts of the Bible) in their own tongue. Before that all had been in Latin, the tongue of the learned. But now Donne could claim that these Psalms could "minister instruction and satisfaction to every man in every emergency and occasion." But is it still possible that the Book of Psalms can do something of that sort for us? Is there to be found in this ancient collection of songs, poems, hymns and meditations anything in the way of spiritual sustenance at all suitable to the needs of today? I believe that there is. Strangely enough Donne once again can tell us why. Later in the same sermon in which he called the Psalms the manna of the Church, he justified his constant recourse to them in preaching because they seemed to him to contain just the kind of mental and spiritual pabulum that the people of England needed to ward off "a new spiritual disease" which was spreading over the length and breadth of the land. This "new disease," he says, "accompanies and complicates almost all bodily diseases with an extraordinary sadness, a predominant melancholy, a faintness of heart and a joylessness of spirit."

It would be difficult to find a more apt description of the kind of mood that has overtaken us once again in this second half of the twentieth century. Some of our rather less elegant phrases describe precisely the same kind of thing. In the early twenties we complained of being "fed up"; in the later thirties, as the Second World War dragged itself along, we complained that we were more than a little "browned off"; while there are many today who frankly confess that they "couldn't care less."

Numberless books have been written attempting to diagnose our trouble, but few seem to offer any prescription whatsoever. This is where the Psalms come in, as I hope to show. A great deal of time and trouble has been spent by scholars in trying to discover the approximate dates at which different individual psalms were written, but very little in the way of positive results has been achieved so far or is ever likely to be. Even if it could be proved that some of them were actually written by David, the traditional "sweet singer of Israel," it would not greatly enhance their value for us, for their great value surely is to be found in the common human experience which they reflect, and that can probably reach us just as well if their authors remain anonymous. The title at the head of some psalm like the third, "*A Psalm of David, when he fled from Absalom his son*," may mean nothing more than that a writer of a much later time wished to describe the feelings of a lonely refugee and took that historic flight of David to give "a local habitation and a name" to his theme, just as a modern poet like Tennyson used the name of Ulysses to describe the feelings of any great adventurer in his old age. Such a device gives a poet more scope and more universality to his poem. It is enough and more than enough for us to know that these Psalms, or "Praises" as they were called in the Hebrew Bible, sprang from that much harassed little nation which has taught mankind more about the faith which can remove mountains than any other. It is indeed better for the Psalms to remain of unknown date and authorship so that they can continue to nourish the spiritual life of every generation, especially one like our own which frankly confesses its spiritual and moral bankruptcy. If H. G. Wells in his old age had been able to turn back to a psalm like the 46th, he might not have uttered his last despairing cry, "Mind at the end of its tether."

But before we look more closely at this "prayerbook of humanity," which is another name for it, we must try to meet the very common difficulty which many people feel and express when they say that they cannot get on with poetry. I don't believe that there is very much in the old objection that it was ruined for them at school because they were condemned to learn a lot of it by heart. Most of us have been able to outgrow that. I think it is more likely to be due to a rather vague subconscious feeling generated by the restlessness and speed of this machine age that anything which does not produce immediate tangible results is utterly useless and irrelevant. At all costs, people will say, we must be practical. But is that really a practical way of approaching life? Darwin, as we mentioned in a previous chapter, didn't think so. He found in his old age that there was something missing and that his capacity for appreciating the non-material side of life had almost disappeared. If he had his life over again, Darwin said, he would devote a little time every week to reading great poetry or listening to good music. I should commend the experience and advice of this great scientist to anyone who has never seriously tried to get on with poetry, especially the poetry of the Psalms which can act as a spiritual make-weight in an age of materialism and can prevent us from getting top-heavy on what we call the "practical" side of life. Is it not just as practical to keep oneself supplied with the power to handle life as it is to increase the wage packet? I have seen many a so-called practical man, successful in business, go all to pieces when confronted by some human situation in which his emotions are involved. Poetry is at one and the same time the expression and the nourishment of the emotional side of our nature, which the Biblical writers speak of as the "heart," though when they use that word they mean to include the intellect as well. *"Thy law is within my heart."* That comes from Psalm 40, which would be a very good Psalm to turn up for a start because it contains so much that is characteristic of the whole collection.

In the first three verses the author tells us of his experience of

God for which he had had to wait a long time but which when it came had lifted him clean out of his depression and frustration and had given him back the balance which he had temporarily lost. Moffatt's translation makes many of these psalms live again by translating the Hebrew into phrases which we use. So verse 2 speaks of the "Slough of despond."

> *"He raised me from a lonesome pit, a muddy bog;*
> *He set my foot on a rock and steadied my steps."*

What was it that had kept this man from God? He tells us in verse 4. It was *"the proud"* and *"such as turn aside to lies,"* that is to say, the self-sufficient and self-satisfied materialists who have "got no use for religion." He, on the other hand, is gratefully aware that God has given him so much to be thankful for that it can't be put into words, for *"they should be more than I am able to express."* In verses 8–10 he tells us that he has found his way to God not along the indirect lines prescribed by the Church of his day but on his own two feet.

> *"Sacrifice and meat-offering thou wouldest not,*
> *but mine ears hast thou opened:*
> *Burnt-offerings and sacrifice for sin hast thou*
> *not required. Then said I, Lo, I come."*

This shows very clearly that the author was well acquainted with the teaching of the great prophets of the eighth century B.C. who had denounced the whole sacrificial system of ancient Israel as being wearisome to God and of no practical moral value to man. This verse is exactly in the same vein as Micah's famous saying:

> *"He hath showed thee, O man, what is good; and what doth the*
> *Lord require of thee, but to do justly, and to love mercy, and to walk*
> *humbly with thy God?"*

It also seems to reflect the teaching of Jeremiah about the the importance and spiritual responsibilities of the individual. But he goes even further than that. He not only heaves a sigh of relief that, thanks to the prophets, all the paraphernalia of priestly mediation has been superseded, but he claims that God's law is no longer an external thing "written and engraven on stone" but an inner authority within each individual soul.

> *"In the volume of the book it is written of me that I should fulfil thy will, O my God: I am content to do it, yea thy law is within my heart."*

To what book can he be referring? Certainly not to the ancient books of the law of Moses, which had all been edited and elaborated in the interests of a priestly religion of observances (including sacrifices), but to the recently published book called Deuteronomy (see Ch. 3) which had been compiled by the disciples of the prophets and which had declared, almost in this Psalmist's own words,

> *"The word is very nigh unto thee, in thy mouth, and in thy heart, that thou mayest do it"* (Deut. 30: 14).

The author of Psalm 50 felt so strongly that this personal religion is the only kind that is worth having that he employed the sharper weapon of satire to expose the absurdity of the outmoded religion of Sacrifices. He says (just as Amos and Isaiah had) that God is tired to death of it all:

> *"I need no bullock from your farms,*
> *no goat out of your herds;*
> *for all the wild things of the wood are mine,*
> *and cattle in their thousands on the hills;*
> *. . ."*

> *"If I were hungry, I would not tell you;*
> *For the whole earth is mine, and all it holds.*
> *Do I eat flesh of bulls?*
> *Do I drink blood of goats?"*

What then does God want from man? The answer of the author of this 50th Psalm is very striking indeed, for he not only says that what God wants is morality (*"pays thy vows unto the Most High"*) but also that we should take him our troubles so that He can help us:

> *"Call upon me in the time of trouble:*
> *I will deliver thee and thou shalt glorify me."*

That brings us to the next great feature of the book of Psalms. God is still thought of as the moral governor of the universe, who "remaineth a King for ever" and "whose judgments are far above out of our sight" (i.e. beyond our full comprehension): of this the Psalmists never lose sight. But what they perceive even more clearly is that God knows and is deeply concerned with the sorrows of the human heart and is *"a very present help in trouble"* (Ps. 46). In fact it is when we are in trouble that we can get to know God best, because that is the moment when He has a very special concern for us. Psalm 31 expresses just that.

"I will be glad and rejoice in thy mercy:
for thou hast considered my trouble;
thou HAST KNOWN MY SOUL IN ADVERSITIES."

That might offer a fresh thought to the man or woman of today, whom one frequently meets, who says "Now this or that has happened to me, I will have no more to do with religion."

But it would be a great mistake to suppose that the Psalmists were religious enthusiasts so carried away with their vision of God as to ignore the great obstacle presented to faith by the problem of suffering. The author of Psalm 73 is acutely conscious of it and, like the author of Job, he finds that there is no satisfactory answer to be found by human reason, especially in the case of the suffering of the righteous when compared with the prosperity and comparative immunity of the wicked. He says, indeed, that it was just this which had nearly undermined his religious faith.

"But as for me, my feet were almost gone;
my steps had well nigh slipped.
For I was envious at the foolish,
when I saw the prosperity of the wicked."

"They are not in trouble as other men;
neither are they plagued like other men."

He had even felt so bitter that he was tempted to charge God with culpable negligence or callous indifference, and to deny the knowledge and care of God for the human soul; but like Job he refused

to give way to these feelings although he felt deeply wounded—
"*It went even through my reins*" (i.e. my whole inner being). The
whole human situation was such a bundle of injustices and inconsistencies that reason was completely baffled.

"*Then thought I to understand this, but it was too hard for me.*"

Should he give it all up and turn atheist? But that would be rank
disloyalty to the family of God ("*Yet, had I meant to utter this aloud,
I had been faithless to thy family*") and, after all, the prosperity of the
wicked is a very transient affair; they will soon "fly forgotten as a
dream"—

> "*like a dream when one awakens,*
> *like phantoms despised by the day*"

—whereas one's relationship with God is the only thing that lasts.

"*Whom have I in heaven but thee?*

> *God is the strength of my heart, and my portion for ever . . .*
> *Thou shalt guide me with thy counsel,*
> *leading me after thyself by the hand.*
> *and after that receive me with glory.*"

His is the same spirit as that of Job when he cried out of the
depths, "*Though he slay me, yet will I trust in Him.*"

But the author of Psalm 73 seems to have travelled further in
thought than the author of Job who thought that he might
possibly catch a fleeting glimpse of God after this life. This
Psalmist evidently believes that he will abide with God for ever.
God will "receive" him "with glory" and will be "his portion for
ever." This, when one comes to think of it, is very remarkable
and must surely represent the belief of many in Israel in the second
and third centuries B.C. It is remarkable because these folk had
evidently arrived at a belief in eternal life without the assistance of
anything in the nature of evidence such as we have in the Resurrection of Jesus Christ from the dead. Indeed, they seem to have
entertained a more real belief in immortality than many conventional and nominal Christians in our own day. Why is this? I

believe it may be because this most precious belief can never rest securely upon external but only upon internal evidence. Here I shall quote some words of Frederick W. Robertson of Brighton. "What is our proof of immortality?" he asks. "Not the Resurrection of Nature from a winter grave or the emancipation of the butterfly. Not even the testimony of the risen dead; for who does not know how shadowy and unsubstantial these intellectual proofs become in unspiritual frames of mind? No, *the life of the Spirit is the evidence . . . he alone can believe in immortality who feels the Resurrection in him already.*" It was surely this personal intimate experience of the communion of the human soul with God, which is reflected in the utterances of these later Psalmists, which enabled them to face the spectres of the mind and to come to rest securely on "the steadfast Rock of immortality," "*the rock that is higher than I.*"

But at this point somebody might possibly raise the objection that all this may be apt to encourage rather an introspective and self-centred kind of religion. Further enquiry into the Book of Psalms will soon correct that impression. They recognise very fully that the root of sin is self-centredness and that the only way to get rid of it is to become more God-centred. Psalm 22 is the finest instance of that. After one of the most woeful lamentations in all literature, the author rises into a hymn of praise:

"*My praise is of thee in the great congregation:*

. . . .

For the kingdom is the Lord's . . .
My seed shall serve him . . . they shall come
and the heavens shall declare his righteousness."

That leads us to notice another and quite different type of psalm like the 104th, the 29th, the 65th or the 8th which are all in praise of God the Creator. When the author of the book of Job pictured God seeking to lift the poor sufferer out of himself, he opened his eyes to the wonder and beauty of the creation. These great Nature psalms do the same thing. The Hebrew title for the book of Psalms is, as I have said, "Praises"; and that is the characteristic note of these Nature psalms.

"Let every thing that hath breath praise the Lord." (150)

*"Praise the Lord, O my soul. O Lord my God, thou
art very great; thou art clothed with honour and majesty.
Who coverest thyself with light as with a garment;
Who stretchest out the heavens like a curtain."* (104)

*"The heavens declare the glory of God; and the
firmament showeth his handywork."* (19)

*"O Lord, how manifold are thy works
In wisdom hast thou made them all:
    the earth is full of thy riches."* (104)

Poets of other nations have dwelt much on the beauty of Nature, but what distinguishes the Hebrew poet is his perception of the "glorious majesty" of God revealed in Nature, especially in its sterner aspects.

It is said that when the children of Israel first encountered the thunders of Sinai, believing that this was the very voice of Deity, they cowered in fear and said, *"Let not God speak to us again lest we die,"* but the attitude of the poet of Psalm 29 is very different. He positively glories in the storm, particularly in the lightning which seems to make the startled forests "skip like a calf" as they are suddenly lit up in the lightning flash and as suddenly plunged back into darkness.

*"The voice of the Lord breaketh the cedars;
Yea, the Lord breaketh the cedars of Lebanon.
He maketh them also to skip like a calf;
Lebanon and Sirion like a young unicorn."* (Probably antelope.)

Moffatt's translation makes it still more clear that Psalm 29 is a description of a tropical thunderstorm:

> *"The voice of the Eternal splits the rocks,
> Splits them with flashes of fire;
> The voice of the Eternal whirls the sand,
> The Eternal whirls the desert of Kadesh.
> The voice of the Eternal twists the trees,
> The voice of the Eternal strips the forest—
> While in his palace all are chanting, 'Glory!'"*

This kind of thing does not come from a people at the beginning of their religion; this psalm shows that they had reached the very much more advanced stage in which they had no difficulty in identifying the God of Nature with the God of grace, for this psalm ends,

> *"The Lord will give strength unto his people;*
> *The Lord will bless his people with peace."*

So he is not only the God who *"maketh the clouds his chariot and walketh upon the wings of the wind"*; He is also the God *"who healeth those that are broken in heart, and giveth medicine to heal their sickness."*

But before closing this chapter in which I have been trying to show the relevance of the Book of Psalms to our lives today, it is necessary to mention something which we often feel to be a serious blot on the Psalmists' escutcheon.

> *"Let their eyes be blinded that they see not, and ever bow down*
>   *their backs . . .*
> *Let their habitation be void and no man dwell in their tents . . .*
> *Let them fall from one wickedness to another . . .*
> *Let them be wiped out of the book of the living and not be written*
>   *among the righteous."*

That extract from Psalm 69 is a fair specimen of the "imprecatory" or cursing psalms. I am of the opinion that none of these should ever be used in Public Worship. It was greatly to the credit of those who produced the Revised prayerbook of 1928 that they put a bracket round the verses which contained them. Surely Christ would treat them as he did the 61st chapter of Isaiah when he stopped short of the phrase *"the day of vengeance."* But as expressions of moral indignation at boiling point they may still have some literary, if not spiritual value. It is at any rate worth noticing that all this eloquent abuse was not levelled at the psalmist's personal enemies but at those whom he felt compelled to regard as the enemies of God, because they were the enemies of justice, mercy and truth. It was against liars and scandal-mongers, calumniators and treacherous rogues who *"grin like a dog and go about the city"*; it was above all against the proud who do not recognise God at all—*"neither is God in all their thoughts"*—that he directed his invective. I think that it probably did these writers more good to write these curses than it can ever do us to read them. But we can hardly claim to be shocked at the feelings of the author of Psalm 137 (written when he was a "displaced person") when he said that he would gladly see Babylonian babies thrown against a wall, when we speak of the massacre of thousands of innocent men, women and children by the atomic bomb as a "military necessity"! The very words we have coined to cover the horror of our deeds, such as "liquidation" or "mopping up operation," are symptomatic of our reluctance to face the stark realities which must ensue when the demoniacal powers of our animal instincts are let loose. Let me again quote from a lecture on peotry given just a hundred years ago to the working men of Brighton by that great and enlightened man, Frederick William Robertson. He claimed that one of the functions of poetry is to relieve pent up feelings. "It is," he said, "a law of our nature that strong feeling, unexpressed either in words or action, becomes morbid. You need not dread the passionate man, whose wrath vents itself in words: dread the man who grows pale and suppresses the language of his resentment. There is something in him yet to come out. This is the secret of England's freedom from revolution and conspiracies: she has free discussion. Wrongs do not smoulder silently, to burst forth unexpectedly. Every grievance may have a hearing, and, not being pent up, spends itself before it is dangerous."

But the poetry of the greatest and best loved psalms like the 23rd, the 19th, the 119th, the 121st, the 103rd, and perhaps above all the 139th, rises far above the level of passion and strong feeling into what Milton calls "the Kingdoms bright of joy and peace," where the soul is face to face with the timeless and the Eternal, and its thirst for the "living God" is satisfied.

> *"If I ascend up into heaven, thou art there:*
> *If I make my bed in hell, behold, thou art there.*

*If I take the wings of the morning, and dwell in the
uttermost parts of the sea,*
*Even there shall thy hand lead me, and thy right hand
shall hold me.*
*If I say, Surely the darkness shall cover me; even the
night shall be light about me.*
*Yea, the darkness hideth not from thee; but the night
shineth as the day: the darkness and the light are
both alike to thee."*

. . . .

*"I will praise thee; for I am fearfully and wonderfully
made:*
*marvellous are thy works; and that my soul knoweth
right well."*

Are we not reading here something which satisfies Shelley's description of true poetry as "the record of the happiest and best moments of the happiest and best minds"?

But more than that.

It is one thing to read the record of a spiritual experience but it is quite another thing to let it nourish and sustain one's soul. Thomas Traherne said something about this which may be taken as a good guide in reading the Psalms. He said, "To consider a thing is to drink it spiritually." Traherne is really challenging us to bring our imagination to bear upon what we read. Now the Psalms were composed by men who believed that the great truths by which we live can be conveyed to us through exposing our imagination to the light which is always streaming in upon us from God—*"In Thy light shall we see light."* The processes of photography suggest the technique of meditation. Focus—Expose —Develop. Take a Psalm like the 23rd. *"The Lord is my shepherd."* Focus on the key words: *"shepherd" "I lack nothing" "He shall feed me" "Green pastures" "He shall convert my soul" "I will fear no evil" "Goodness and mercy shall follow me" "for ever."*

Expose the mind, which may be compared with a sensitive film, to the light which is in those phrases, and give thanks for it. *"Praise the Lord, O my soul!" "I will yet give thee thanks, who art the help of my countenance and my God.*" Then take that half-developed thought with you into the hurly-burly of the day, and you will find that it comes back again and again; not like a recurring tune of which we tire, but fresh every time, like the manna which was gathered before the first dew of morning had left it.

CHAPTER EIGHT

A Book for Those Who Can Believe but Little

ON the flyleaf of the first Bible which I ever possessed, and which has long since disappeared, there was inscribed a text which has never been far from my mind; I can see it now in my father's copper-plate handwriting:

*"WHATSOEVER THY HAND FINDETH TO DO,
DO IT WITH THY MIGHT"* (Ecclesiastes 9: 10).

It was the custom in those days (1896) to pick out a single verse or, as in this case, half a verse from any book of the Bible and thus imprint it for ever on a child's mind. That way of handling scripture had one advantage, but one only. It familiarised children with the actual words of the Bible. But of course it could at the same time be very misleading if it gave one the impression, as it was almost bound to do, that the text chosen was really representative of the message to mankind which the original author of the book from which it was taken wished to convey. Still more unfortunate was it when the words selected came from the earlier parts of the Old Testament and reflected a primitive belief. I remember for instance a bereaved parent whose only son had just been killed on a motor bicycle saying with indignation, "I suppose I loved him too much and so God took him out of jealousy." When I told her not to talk nonsense, she replied at once by quoting words from the second commandment in Exodus 20—*"I, the Lord thy God, am a jealous God"*—and added, "That's what the good book says, doesn't it?"

No, it is a fatal misuse of the "Book of books" to treat it as you would a book by a single author. The different books of the Old Testament, as we have seen, represent the thoughts of the Hebrew people at many different periods in their history and therefore often reflect points of view about God and life and morals which were subsequently corrected as knowledge widened and experience deepened.

74

Now, as I said a moment ago, the verse which my father inscribed on the flyleaf of my first Bible was only half a verse, and he probably had a very good reason for not quoting the other half, which is this:

> *"for there is no work, nor device, nor knowledge nor wisdom in the grave, whither thou goest."*

As a Christian, he could heartily recommend *"Whatsoever thy hand findeth to do, do it with thy might"* as an excellent maxim, but he certainly could not accept as a sound one the original author's reason for teaching it. Every thinker or writer, whether biblical or non-biblical, is necessarily limited by the beliefs current in his day; and the greatest limitation under which the author of the book of Ecclesiastes laboured was that he, like most of his contemporaries, believed that there is no life at all beyond the grave. Does that mean that his book has no value for the Christian reader who believes in "the life everlasting"? Far from it. The belief in immortality, as we have seen in dealing with the Psalms, had only just begun to take root in the minds of a few poets and mystics who were a bit ahead of their times. Furthermore, it is still true that even after nearly 2000 years of Christianity there are thousands to whom the thought of a hereafter of any kind means practically nothing. I am sure that there are many preachers of today who forget this, especially in their Easter sermons and also at Funeral Services. What is often given on such occasions goes clean over the heads of ninety per cent of their listeners, because the preacher is apt to assume that the belief in immortality which he holds is held by all men. And it is not. Therefore the book of Ecclesiastes—which was written by someone who calls himself "The Preacher" (or more accurately "The Professor," for that is the true translation of "Quoheleth," the Hebrew title of the book) and who had no such belief—may surely be a book of great value to those who, as the title of this chapter suggests, can believe but little. As a matter of fact, the book of Ecclesiastes only got into the Canon of Scripture by the skin of its teeth, though not because its author disbelieved in the hereafter but for other reasons. At the second synod of the Council of Jamnia (when the canon of

Scripture was closed) opinion as to whether or not it should be admitted as "Scripture" was sharply divided. The Rabbis of the more conservative school of Shammai objected to it on account of its inconsistencies (which are very obvious), while those of the more liberal school of Hillel managed to secure its acceptance because of its natural piety, possibly because of its noble ending:

> *"This is the end of the matter; all hath been heard. Fear God, and keep his commandments: for this is the whole duty of man."*

We can be very thankful that the more liberal Rabbis succeeded in winning the day, for as a modern commentator has said, "there is room in the Bible for all phases of life." The language and style of the book, which actually contains numerous words only found in later Hebrew literature, are sufficient proof that it has nothing whatever to do with the times, much less with the pen, of King Solomon. The statement, "I the Preacher was King over Israel in Jerusalem" (1: 12) is obviously not a statement of fact but is one more instance of the literary device, quite common in the Bible, used by an anonymous writer to secure a hearing. Just as David was the traditional father of Psalmody, so Solomon was the traditional father of Wisdom, and though the author of Ecclesiastes may have been the first to use the great King's name, he was far from being the last. (A later book which didn't get into the Canon, and was written much later, bears the title "The Wisdom of Solomon.")

He was also no doubt very glad to use such a reputable *nom de plume* to protect himself against conservative critics who would certainly disapprove of some of his rather unconventional opinions. Indeed, so unconventional are they that another modern writer has given the book the title, "The Confessions of an Adventurous Soul." To begin with, "The Professor," as we will now speak of him, does not use the name "Jehovah" for God, for "Jehovah" is the God who reveals himself to man, the God of the Prophets, the God who speaks. He uses "Elohim," the moral but impersonal Deity who hides himself, the great First Cause whose plans and purposes *"Man may never fathom."* It would not be fair to call the Professor an agnostic, as some people have, because he obviously holds some quite definite beliefs about God, as his last words declare, "*God shall bring every work into judgment, with every hidden thing, whether it be good, or whether it be evil.*" Yet there is a strain of what we might call reverent Agnosticism all the way through his book.

> "*As thou knowest not what is the way of the wind, nor how the bones do grow in the womb of her that is with child: even so thou knowest not the works of God who maketh all*" (11: 5).

His opening soliloquy reflects very clearly that he lived not in the heyday of the nation's prosperity, the golden age of Solomon "in all his glory," when a queen who came from afar to visit Jerusalem could declare that the half was not told her, but in that time when the poverty stricken Jews who had returned from the Babylonian exile had fallen under the tyranny and oppression of their Persian masters. It was a time (to quote his own words) "when you see the poor being oppressed . . . right and justice being tampered with in the state . . . one official preying on another" (5: 8). Under such circumstances the Professor has no hope whatever for the future prosperity, or even the reasonable well-being, of his nation. All he can do is to write something to help a despairing, disillusioned people to be realists, to accept life as it is and take it as it comes, not to expect too much and above all to make the most of what remains to be enjoyed. That goes a long way to account for the sombre tone in which he writes "*Man labours at his toil under the sun: what does he gain? . . . all things are full of weariness . . . vanity of vanities, all is vanity.*" That is not just pessimism, as it has often been taken to be. It is his way of showing his readers that he fully understands their mood and that he shares it with them. It is as if he were saying, 'I frankly admit that you and I have struck a bad patch in history and nothing we do seems worth while. Life is bleak and disappointing; all the zest has gone out of it. But supposing that we were all as rich as King Solomon, should we be any happier? You think we should all then be as happy as the great king? But should we? Let us see.'

The Professor then takes it upon himself to address his readers as though he were Solomon—Solomon the rich but also Solomon the wise and, towards the end of the book, Solomon the man who reverenced and worshipped God. Hence his words, "*I the Preacher was King in Jerusalem,*" really mean, 'This is what the great wise king, whose golden age you look back to with wistful regret, would be saying to you now.'

Chapter 2 is a vivid description of the quest for happiness. "Solomon" had tried everything in the way of what men call pleasure—wine, women and song; magnificent country houses, landscape gardening, orchards and artificial lakes. He became a connoisseur in treasures of gold and silver. He had stud farms, a harem and a private orchestra to boot. "*Nothing,*" he says, "*did I refuse myself. I denied my heart no joy.*" Yet when he came to take stock of it all, it turned to dust and ashes in his hand: "*But when I turned to look at all I had achieved and at all my toil and trouble, then it was all vain and futile.*"

Chapter 3 tells how, having given up the search for happiness among material things, he tried to find satisfaction in evolving a philosophy of life with a view to improving the state of things in this world. But this too ended in failure. 'Search as you will, search where you will,' he says in effect, 'it's no use imagining that you can change the mysterious alternations of peace and war, love and hate, birth and death. Neither is it any use to try and explain anything, "*for the mind of man God has appointed mystery, so that man may never fathom God's own purpose from beginning to end.*" The whole thing's baffling.'

This of course is getting very near fatalism. In fact the poor Professor (impersonating King Solomon) often wishes he were dead or that he had never been born.

"*I looked again,*" he says, "*and saw all the oppression that goes on in the world . . . and I judged the dead already in their graves to be more happy than the living . . . yes, and happier than them both the man unborn, who has never known the misery that goes on in the world.*"

If he had left it at that, the book would have little value beyond the graphic picture that it gives of the futility of materialism, but there is something much more than this. In Chapter 5 there is sudden and abrupt change. We have followed him right down into the Slough of Despond and it looked as if he were going to sink into the abyss of fatalism, when to our utter amazement we find that he has conducted us to the house of God and bids us go in with him.

"Never enter God's house carelessly; draw near him to listen, and then your service is better than what fools offer—for all a fool knows is how to do wrong."

So after having tried all that life has to offer, this man of the world turns like the Psalmist to the sanctuary of God, hoping to understand life a little better there. He has nothing of the intense feeling of fellowship with the living God which the Psalmist had. In fact he feels that silence is better than speech, for *"God is in heaven, and thou upon earth: therefore let thy words be few,"* and *"Be not rash with thy mouth."*

Public worship, as he understands it, has no virtue in itself. It all depends on the attitude of the worshipper. He would have no use at all for wordy prayers or for the kind of prayers which offer information to the Almighty, or for a sentimental flow of words with nothing behind them. *"Never say to God, 'I vowed that by mistake,' lest God be angry at your excuse and undo you. Stand in awe of God for many dreams and words mean many a vain folly"* (5: 6, 7).

How many modern agnostics get as far as that? He at any rate makes the venture. After all his experiments with life and in spite of all his doubts, this worldling has never quite lost what Dr. Schweitzer (the missionary to the outcasts of Africa) calls "Reverence for life."

From this point (Chap. 5) onwards the Professor allows us to see the effect which the little religion he has been able to hold on to has upon his judgment and his character.

First, *"A good name is better than precious ointment"* (7: 1) (in other words, character is more important than wealth and possessions) and *"wisdom is as good as an inheritance"* (7: 11). Then, happiness is not, as he once thought, the be-all and end-all of life: happiness is a by-product. *"In prosperous days enjoy yourself, but in evil days ponder this, that the one is the doing of God as well as the other"* (7: 14). That leads him to give a counsel of moderation in all things.

> *"Be not righteous overmuch;*
> *Neither make thyself overwise."*

Is this not his way of warning people against self-righteousness and intellectual snobbishness and against egotism which is at the root of both? I think that is a valid interpretation of his words, because he follows it up with, *"Why shouldest thou destroy thyself?"* Is there anything so destructive of personality as egotism? This chapter also shows how he has begun to think more of other people's troubles than of his own. That is why he says that *"it is better to go to the house of mourning than to the house of feasting"* (7: 2) and that *"sorrow is better than laughter,"* for *"sadness does the heart good."* Is he not in these short pithy sentences beginning to get to grips with the mysteries of life which he still humbly confesses are beyond him, as they are beyond us? Who knows but that it may have been through meditating upon such words that Christ a few centuries later declared, *"Blessed are they that mourn, for they shall be comforted"*? We know well enough that it is easier to forget oneself and one's own sorrows by going, as the Professor recommends, to "the house of mourning" rather than to "the house of feasting." Dante, too, may have been thinking along the same lines when he said, "Sorrow remarries us to God." The Professor at any rate seems to have had something of that experience and so felt a better man. He is certainly now, if still a sad man, a wiser man. Years and experience have told. But still progress towards the good life is a slow and uneven business and the Professor does not hide that fact from us, for his seventh chapter containing, as we have seen, all this great improvement in his judgment, concludes with a strangely crude opinion. Suddenly and abruptly he becomes dogmatic and leaps to a general conclusion upon a matter about which surely nobody ought to generalize or be dogmatic:

> *"One true man in a thousand,*
> *but never a true woman."* (7: 29)

It is true that he wishes to warn us against the designing woman "whose heart is a net" and whose "clasp is a chain" (7: 26). No doubt in his earlier days he had suffered from that kind of woman —and of course the worthy man had no idea that his writings would ever become "Holy Scripture"—but he can hardly have paid much attention to the grand idyll of Isaac and Rebecca, which must have been known to him. Possibly the famous description in the Book of Proverbs (Ch. 31) of the virtuous woman —who, besides getting up before dawn to feed her household, "talks shrewd sense and offers kindly counsel"—may have been written to confound him. (The Book of Proverbs may be a contemporary writing.) In reading such a passage one must, of course, heed the advice offered by the Doctrinal Commission (1938) on the exposition of Scripture, when it was declared that the "supreme spiritual value of some parts of the Bible is not shared by all." So let us read on quickly through Chapters 8, 9 and 10 in which the Professor summarises the results of his observation of human nature and of life and advises us to accept what God gives us in the way of happiness and to make the most of it, however bad the times in which one lives may be.

"*Anyone still alive has something to live for; even a live dog is better than a dead lion.*"

As he grows older, his nature seems to be mellowing; perhaps his son's experience of women was better than his.

"*Enjoy life with the woman whom you love, through all the fleeting life which God has given you in this world, for this is what you are meant to get out of your life of toil under the sun*" (9: 9).

That and the noble maxim "*Whatsoever thy hand findeth to do, do it with thy might,*" which we quoted at the beginning, prepares us for his grand conclusion in Chapters 11 and 12. The tone of these final chapters is so noble and exalted by comparison with the rest of the book that some scholars have suggested that it comes from another hand than that which wrote "*Vanity of vanities, all is vanity.*" But I see no reason for this. Is it not much more natural to see the Professor who has found the spring tantalising because it is so brief, and the summer wearisome and arid, reaching at last his Indian Summer and, recalling something of the joy and zest of youth, addressing his grandchildren:

"*Remember now thy Creator in the days of thy youth.*"

His reverent agnosticism has all but passed into a living faith. His words, "*Cast thy bread upon the waters: for thou shalt find it after many days,"* are something more than merely prudential counsel. *"Divide a portion into seven, yea even into eight"* means something more than "minimise your risks: don't put all your eggs in one basket." The Hebrew expression, which is the same as that in Job 5: 19 (*"He shall deliver thee in six troubles, yea in seven there shall be no evil touch thee"*) is not arithmetical but poetic. It means a glorious prodigality, as contrasted with cautious prudence, like the "seventy times seven" forgiveness. After all, he reflects, how little we really know; therefore let us take a comfort from our ignorance and give God not simply the benefit of the doubt but the trust which is his due.

"*Thou knowest not the works of God who maketh all.*"

What we do know of God's works is wonderful enough to encourage us to trust his wisdom in guiding, perhaps even in prospering, the enterprises and ventures we make in good faith. It is like the Psalmist's reflection:

"*They that sow in tears shall reap in joy.
He that now goeth on his way weeping,
But beareth forth good seed,
Shall doubtless come again rejoicing,
Bringing his sheaves with him.*"   (Psalm 126)

It may even have unconsciously inspired a modern scientist to write, "How do we know what anything means to us, who can see nothing—not even a flower—from God's side, through His far-seeing eyes. All we know is that these things are all partial manifestations of Him in us—that the beauty of the stars and the fury of the storm, that the loveliness of the lily and the loathsomeness of disease, that the radiancy of life and the mystery of death, that joy and tragedy, are all fragmentary expressions of something in its full meaning and entirety infinitely divine." (*Faiths and Heresies of a Poet and Scientist*. R. C. McFie Williams & Norgate.)

The poet Doddridge seems to have caught his spirit:

" 'Live while you live,' the Epicure would say,
'And seize the pleasure of the present day.'
'Live while you live,' the sacred Preacher cries,
'And give to God each moment as it flies.' "

It has not been always thus with him, as he has told us in the earlier part of his book, but now he implores the young not to repeat his mistakes, *"for all these things God will bring thee into judgment."*

This counsel is repeated in the sublime yet sombre poem of the 12th and final chapter, which stands quite alone in the world's literature. Here all the richness of Hebrew imagery is employed to describe what most of our western writers have regarded as revolting and gruesome—old age and death. We might well contrast it with Shakespeare's *King Lear*, who cries,

"Pray do not mock me:
I am a very foolish, fond old man,
Four score and upward, not an hour more or less,
And, to deal plainly,
I fear I am not in my perfect mind."

Our Professor on the other hand, although he knows that his faculties of sight and hearing and locomotion are beginning to fail him, can still make music of it all: he "makes music out of life's remainders."

The picture in his mind is that of a grand old mansion which has once witnessed scenes of unrivalled mirth and revelry, hospitality and industry, slowly crumbling to ruin. One should read it in the matchless prose of the Authorised Version for atmosphere but in Moffatt's translation to get the sense and to appreciate the sublety of the imagery. I will go further and contrast his description of old age and death with the trite and crude phrases which we commonly use. Bearing in mind the picture of the fine mansion or castle gradually falling into decay, we will put our phrases alongside his.

Our Phrases	*Those of the Professor*
The old man is pretty shaky on his pins.	When the guards tremble in the house of Life, when its upholders bow.
He's a toothless old man.	The maids that grind are few and fail.
His eyes are bleary.	Ladies at the lattice lose their lustre.
He's deaf as a post.	The doors to the street are shut, and the sound of the mill runs low.

He's losing his voice.	The twitter of birds is faint, and dull the daughters of song.
He gets giddy.	Old age fears a height, and even a walk has its terrors.
He died.	The silver cord is snapped and the golden lamp drops broken, the pitcher breaks at the fountain, the wheel breaks at the cistern.

But is death the end, as he used to think in his earlier days? It may be that, like Victor Hugo, when "winter is upon his head" ("*his hair is almond white*") "eternal spring is in his heart and the nearer he approaches the end the plainer does he hear the immortal symphonies of the world to come." We must not read too much into his last words, but have they not a noble hint or intimation of personal immortality?

> "*Then shall the dust return to the earth as it was,*
> *And the spirit return unto God who gave it.*"

CHAPTER NINE

The Gospel in the Old Testament

WHEN a traveller visiting Switzerland for the first time in his life is confronted with the spectacle of the great central mountain peaks of the Bernese Oberland, he feels his inmost soul hushed into an awed silence before the grandeur of those three giants, the Jungfrau, the Monch, and the Eiger. It is a vision to lift the spirit into a strangely rarefied atmosphere, far above all trivial things. The Old Testament is like that. From the lowlands of man's original primitive thoughts of God, there rise the foothills of inspired glimpses of the truth, until suddenly there bursts upon the reader all the splendour, all the breathtaking majesty of a vision so glorious that its image must remain stamped upon the mind for ever after. And this spiritual Jungfrau of the Old Testament writings is the latter part of the book of Isaiah.

I am thinking of Chapters 40–66. Scholars have for some time now been of the opinion that we have here two separate books, Chapters 40–55 and Chapters 56–66 (the latter coming from a third Isaiah), but for our present purpose I shall treat Chapters 40–66 as a whole. The first thirty-nine chapters (with the exception of Chapters 24–27, which are the work of a much later writer) come from Isaiah the statesman-prophet of the eighth century; but from 40 onwards (certainly 40–55) we are reading the message of an unknown prophet of the Exile, whom we shall speak of as the "Second Isaiah." The opening words of the 40th Chapter make that perfectly clear, and the mention of Cyrus the Persian conqueror of Babylon (44: 28 and 45: 1), by whose conquest the exiles were liberated and allowed to return to Palestine, establishes the date of the book beyond a doubt.

There is no book in the Old Testament which has lent itself to so much exposition by the scholar or has supplied a theme for so many Christian hymns—from William Cowper's famous "Hark my soul, it is the Lord" to Samuel Johnson's "City of God"—as this collection of writings which I have ventured to call "The

Gospel in the Old Testament." Professor R. G. Moulton who gave us *The Modern Reader's Bible* (the Bible classified and arranged in literary form) thought so highly of it simply as a literary masterpiece, quite apart from its religious teaching, that it ought, he says, to "take its place with the book of Job beside Plato and Homer in the curricula of our schools and colleges." Moulton further wrote, "It may be safely asserted that nowhere else in the literature of the world have so many colossally great ideas been brought together within the limits of a single work." Viewing Second Isaiah then as a whole, we can pick out three main themes which belong together just like the Jungfrau, the Monch, and the Eiger in the Bernese Oberland. These three themes, which are quite inseparable from each other, are:

> God the Redeemer.
> Man the idolater who is always cherishing false pictures of God.
> Man the servant of the God who is afflicted in the afflictions of man.

In his introduction to a book with the arresting title, "Your God is too Small," (Epworth Press) Mr. J. B. Phillips writes, "No one is ever really at ease in facing what we call 'life' and 'death' without a religious faith. The trouble with many modern people today is that they have not found a God big enough for modern needs While their experience of life has grown in a score of directions and their mental horizons have been expanded to the point of bewilderment by world events and by scientific discoveries, their ideas of God have remained static." It was not the fashion in Second Isaiah's day to write an introduction to one's book (although in the Bible there is the one exception of St. Luke who wrote a preface to his "Gospel" and to his other work, The Acts of the Apostles); but if it had been, Mr. Phillips' introductory words are just the kind of thing Second Isaiah might have written. The Israelites had gone away into exile in the sixth and seventh centuries B.C. with a conception of God which was, in spite of the teaching of the great Prophets, far too small. The first Isaiah had tried to stretch their minds and to lift them from the idea of a deity who was supposed to enjoy the smell of sacrifice and incense to the conception of a God who demands holiness of life. But with all the widening of their experience in other lands, they came back in the fifth century B.C. with much the same old ideas.

There is always a more important question than, "Do you believe in God?" and that is, "What kind of a God do you believe in?" It is quite obvious that the returned exiles still regarded the Exile as the direct punishment of God for their national apostacy. This was the first matter upon which our prophet has something vital to say. He starts—and here is his greatness—as a true teacher must always start, just where they stand. He does not start off by denying outright the idea of punishment; for if he had, the little grain of truth in that rather crude thought might easily have been lost. He begins by telling them that if they are still feeling sore and their minds are still smarting with a sense of injustice or abandonment, God is with them, not as a judge but as a healer.

> *"Comfort ye, comfort ye my people, saith your God. Speak ye comfortably to Jerusalem, and cry unto her that her warfare* ('time of conscription') *is accomplished, that her iniquity is pardoned* ('her guilt is paid off'): *for she hath received from the Lord's hand full punishment for all her sins"* (40: 1–2).

> *"I, even I, am he that blotteth out thy transgressions for my own sake, and will not remember thy sins"* (i.e. I put your sins out of my mind) (43: 25).

> *"O Israel, thou shalt not be forgotten of me. I have blotted out, as a thick cloud, thy transgressions and, as a cloud, thy sins; return unto me; for I have redeemed thee"* (44: 21).

Notice the unutterable tenderness of the imagery in these next words: *"Can a woman forget her sucking child, that she should not have compassion on the son of her womb? Yea, they may forget, yet will I not forget thee"* (A.V. 49: 15). *"Look, Sion, I have printed your walls plain on both my hands!—your ruins are before me all the time"* (Moffat 49: 16).

87

7

We at once recall Cowper's lines which were inspired by these verses.

> "Can a woman's tender care
> Cease towards the child she bare?
> Yes, she may forgetful be,
> Yet will I remember thee.
>
> Mine is an unchanging love,
> Higher than the heights above,
> Deeper than the depths beneath,
> Free and faithful, strong as death."

It is not until he has brought God right down into the very arena of their woes that he begins to try and explain to them the true value of these days when, after the first thrill of the home-coming, nothing seems to be happening and they are just marking time.

> "Why do you complain, O Jacob, why do you cry, O Israel,
> 'My fate the Eternal never notices, my rights are unregarded
>   by my God?'
> Come now! Do you not understand, have you not heard,
> That the Eternal is an everlasting God,
> The maker of the world from end to end?
> He never faints, never is weary,
> His insight is unsearchable;
> Into the weary he puts power,
> And adds new strength to the weak.
> Young men may faint and weary,
> The strong youths may give way,
> But those who wait for the Eternal shall renew their strength,
> They put out wings like eagles,
> They run and never weary,
> They walk and never faint."   (40: 27–31, Moffatt)

I have quoted this in full so that even if the reader has not yet got his Bible off the shelf he may be able to see and ponder some of the greatest words ever written about God—the God who is with his children not simply when they are, so to speak, on the crest of the wave or when they feel that they can do a sprint, but when life seems to have slowed down to an everyday humdrum walk. *"They shall walk and not faint."* Is not this God of the Commonplace the God who can meet and satisfy our human needs? Yes, but only on condition that man is growing up spiritually. These great thoughts of God cannot reach him so long as smaller thoughts stand in the way. To go back to our mountaineering simile, one often finds that quite a small foothill will hide the majestic peaks from our sight. So Isaiah issues his warning:

> *"My thoughts are not your thoughts,*
> *Neither are your ways my ways, saith the Lord.*
> *For as the heavens are higher than the earth,*
> *So are my ways higher than your ways,*
> *And my thoughts than your thoughts."* (55: 8–9)

Second Isaiah is the first prophet to give us that tremendously important truth, so often ignored or forgotten, that our very highest thoughts of God are after all only human and finite. As Tennyson said,

> "Sooner earth might go round heaven,
> And the strait girth of time enswathe the fullness of eternity,
> Than language grasp the Infinite of Love."

If man forgets that, he will always be worshipping something less than God, something that must inevitably shut out the true God from his vision; in short, an idol of some kind. (The word idol is Greek "eidōlon"—a picture.) So an idol is not necessarily something made of wood or stone, silver or gold, but may be just a false picture treasured and cherished in the mind. One of the last words in the New Testament is, *"Little children, keep yourselves from idols"* (I John). This is so great a danger to the soul of man in every age and clime and in every religion that Isaiah devotes a good deal of space to it in the fortieth, forty-fourth and forty-sixth Chapters. Here Moffatt's translation of Chapter 44: 9–20 brings out the writer's meaning much more clearly than the Authorised Version. The passage is an interesting description of the making of an actual idol of wood and iron, but it is applicable also to the false ideas of God which men in their folly still make for themselves.

> "*Makers of idols are all inane, and their adored images are futile; an idol's devotees are blind and dull, their end is shame. Who would ever carve a god or cast an idol?—mere futilities! The spells put on it make a sorry show, and its magic charms are only man-made.*"

We then have his graphic description of an idol factory.

> "The blacksmith works with the coals and hammers the idol into shape, plying his brawny arms, losing strength as he grows hungry, and weary for a drink of water. *The worker in wood draws lines on the block, marking them with a pencil; then he shapes the idol with his plane into a human figure, comely as a man, to occupy a shrine. In cutting timber for this purpose a man will fix upon some plane or oak, which God planted and the rain nourished to serve as fuel; men kindle a fire with it to warm themselves, or start a blaze in order to bake bread.* But he turns it into a god for worship; he makes it into an idol and bows down to it! Half of it he burns in the fire, roasting flesh upon the embers; he eats the roast meat and *he is satisfied, warming himself and saying, 'Ha, I am warm now, I feel the glow!'* The other half he turns into a god, into an idol, and bows down to it, worshipping it, praying to it, crying, 'Save me, for you are my god!'"

The words *in italics* are specially interesting. In them Isaiah is exposing not so much the wickedness as the stupidity of idolatry. Fancy making such a stupid mistake about the use of a tree!

> "*Such men are ignorant and senseless, their eyes are bedaubed till they cannot see, and their minds are closed to knowledge;* none of them calls to mind—none has sense and wit enough to say to himself, 'Half of it I burned in the fire, baking bread upon its embers and roasting meat for food; and am I to make the other half into a horrid idol? Am I to bow down to a wooden block?'"

And here is the delusion and self-deception of all forms of idolatry, whether material or mental.

> "*Ashes will satisfy a man who is so duped by a delusion that he cannot pull himself up by asking, 'Am I not holding to something false and vain?'*"

This book is not a commentary or an exposition, so I must resist the strong temptation to enlarge upon this matter. I would only ask the reader to consider the application of Isaiah's description of the idol factory to the idols we are still in the habit of making in the modern world—Money, Happiness, Science, and many another—and to verify the prophet's verdict in our own experience of the disillusionment and the feelings of frustration and futility which are so characteristic of our time. Look then, by contrast, at the superb picture of God which he gives:

> *"Thus saith the Lord, The heaven is my throne and the earth my footstool. What manner of house will ye build me? And what shall be the place of my rest? For all these things hath mine hand made, and so all things came to be.* (66)
>
> *"Thus saith the high and lofty One that inhabiteth eternity, whose name is Holy; I dwell in the high and holy place, with him also that is of a contrite and humble spirit, to revive the spirit of the humble, and to revive the heart of the contrite ones . . . I have seen his ways, and will heal him; I will lead him also, and restore comforts unto him. . . . Peace, peace to him that is far off, and to him that is near."* (57)

As man's thoughts of God are stretched in this way, he will find that his ideas about himself and his place in God's scheme of things will undergo a similar change.

This brings us in sight of the two companion peaks which Isaiah challenges us to contemplate: Man as the servant of God; man the willing and obedient burden-bearer of the world's adversity, sorrows and sufferings. In presenting this, Second Isaiah takes up and enlarges and deepens some of the thoughts of his great predecessor (Isaiah of the eighth century, 1–39) about the "Man" or the "Messiah" who is to bring Israel and the world "the salvation of God." He could not adopt this hope in its earlier forms because they were too nationalistic. In its original form the hope of a Messiah or deliverer was concentrated upon a Kingly figure, a prince of the house of David, who would not only deliver the nation from its enemies but "smite in sunder the heads over divers countries." The author of Psalm 2 looked forward to one who would rule the heathen (all non-Jews) with "a rod of iron, and break them in pieces like a potter's vessel." As the modern poet has sung,

> "They all were looking for a king to slay their foes and
>   set them high."

It was upon this kind of Warrior Messiah that the hopes of the returned exiles were fixed. That explains the rigorist intolerance of foreign marriages, against which the author of the book of Ruth protested. Therefore Second Isaiah makes it very clear that, while he is thinking of a Messiah, it is a very different kind of Messiah upon whom he sets his hopes.

> "The Eternal now says, '*Tis too slight a service to set the clans of Jacob up again, and restore Israel's survivors; I now appoint you to bring light to the nations, that my salvation may reach the world's end*" (49: 6).

The germ of this more emancipated conception of Messiah was there in the mind of the first Isaiah:

> "*On him shall rest the spirit of the Eternal, the spirit of wisdom and insight, the spirit of counsel and strength, the spirit that knows and reverences the Eternal. He will not judge by appearances, nor decide by hearsay, but will act with justice to the helpless and decide fairly for the humble*" (Isa: 11).

That is to say, Messiah will not be a warrior prince of the house of David, but an inspired leader of mankind. This shows itself still more clearly in Chapter 32: 2–4. "*And a man shall be as an hiding place from the wind, and a covert from the tempest; as rivers of water in a dry place, as the shadow of a great rock in a weary land.*"

It is the idea of this stalwart, wise, inspired, type of Messiah that comes to full flower in the mind of the Prophet whom we call the Second Isaiah. He has shed all his royalty and pomp and circumstance. He is also quite free from the supernatural trappings with which he is encumbered in the writings of that later school of thought known to scholars as "Apocalyptic," of which the book of Daniel is a specimen, where he is expected to appear "on the clouds of heaven." The Messiah of the Second Isaiah is simply described as a servant. We have no difficulty in distinguishing the passages relating to him, because they all begin, *"Behold my servant."* The main passages are to be found in Isaiah 41: 8–10, Isaiah 42: 1–9, Isaiah 49: 1–6, Isaiah 50: 4–10, and the best known passage of all 52: 13 to 53: 12.

This conception of the "Man" who is the hope not simply of Israel but of the whole world was not possible—and still is not possible—so long as God is tied up with the tribe or the nation. If you are always expecting God to help your nation to overcome its enemies, if God remains, as he still does in some people's minds, "Lord of our far-flung battle line," your nation will never become a truly missionary nation, and God will never be able to come into action for the salvation of all mankind, but only for the destruction of your enemies. It was this that Second Isaiah was the first to see and teach.

But how is God going to act? Not through some violent political or supernatural "break through" such as contemporaries were looking for, but quietly, slowly and unobtrusively. *"Behold my servant, whom I uphold"* (Isa. 42). This is the kind of personality through whom God is going to act.

"I have put my spirit upon him" (he is truly inspired) *"to carry true religion to the nations."* (Israel is to be a missionary nation.) He will not use any of the conventional methods of an evangelistic campaign.

> *"He shall not be loud and noisy, he shall not*
> *shout in public;*
> *He shall not crush a broken reed nor quench a*
> *wick that dimly burns;*
> *Loyally shall he set forth true religion,*
> *He shall not be broken nor grow dim,*
> *Till he has settled true religion upon earth,*
> *Till far lands long for his instruction."* (42: 1–4)

In the next passage (Isa. 50: 4–10) the servant is described as one who listens for his instructions day by day.

> *"Morning by morning he awakens me*
> *to learn my lesson,*
> *And never have I disobeyed, or turned away."*

This practice of listening prayer is the practical application of the great promise of the Book of Deuteronomy (30: 14).

> *"The word is very near to you, it is on your lips and in your mind, to be obeyed."*

This obedience will often involve God's servant in persecution and suffering for the truth which it is his duty to proclaim.

> *"I let them lash my back, and pluck my beard out;*
> *I never hid my face from shame and spitting."*

This inevitable suffering in the cause of true religion becomes more and more prominent when we read on to the final and best known passages in Chapters 52 and 53, until it becomes at length not his misfortune but his crowning glory and, indeed, the chief weapon of God's converting and healing power. This patient, unembittered endurance of suffering for righteousness sake, says the prophet, is going to be the eighth wonder of the world:

> *"They shall see what they were never told, a sight unheard of.*
> *'Who could have believed,' they cry, 'what we have heard?*
> *Whoever had the Eternal's power so revealed to them?'"*

Now we are sure that this prophet is thinking not of an individual sufferer but of his nation, for the description of the part he is to play in the redemption of the world begins,

> *"Why, Israel of old grew like a sapling,*
> *like a shoot springing from dry soil;*
> *he had no beauty to attract our eyes,*
> *no charm to make us choose him—*
> *disfigured till he seemed a man no more,*
> *deformed out of the semblance of a man.*
> He was despised and shunned by men,
> *a man of pain, who knew what sickness was;*
> *. . . he was despised, we took no heed of him."*

In those words the prophet is describing what the great nations like Egypt and Assyria and Persia must have thought of poor little Israel, which never in all its stormy history ever occupied a territory bigger than that of Wales. Yet now, he says, the nations are going to have the surprise of their lives. God is going to use the mighty spirit of endurance and patience under unmerited suffering of this despised people for the conversion of a world which will eventually, and in the very long run, acknowledge its debt. In wonder and awe they will exclaim,

> *"Yet ours was the pain he bore, the sorrow he endured!*
> *We thought him suffering from a stroke at God's own hand;*
> *Yet he was wounded because we had sinned,*
> *'twas our misdeeds that crushed him;*
> *'twas for our welfare that he was chastised,*
> *the blows that fell to him have brought us healing."*

So the prophet speaks the last word of the Old Testament on the mystery and problem of suffering, and it may be taken, as it undoubtedly was taken by Christ who read and pondered deeply on all the words we have quoted, as the foundation of our Christian philosophy of suffering. Let Dr. Streeter interpret this for us. "Few things," he says, "avail to inspire and re-create the human heart as does the spectacle of crushing misfortune cheerfully and heroically borne; the unconscious influence which those who act thus exert is far greater than they or others comprehend. Here is the element of truth in the common talk about the ennobling and purifying power of suffering; though it is not the suffering, but the way it is borne, that ennobles. Pain not just submitted to, but willingly accepted, makes the sufferer socially creative. A man counts in this world to the extent that he has thought and to the extent that he has felt, provided always that he has thought and felt in the right way. Suffering rightly borne is constructive work. He who has 'borne his bit' has also 'done his bit'; pain conquered is power" (*Reality*, p. 249).

I have nothing to add to that except to ask the reader to carry this Gospel of the Old Testament in his mind as we move forward now out of the Old Testament into the New, where the ideal of the suffering servant, never accepted by the nation of Israel, became the inspiration of Jesus, the Son of Man, the Hope and Saviour of the world.

THE AUTHORSHIP OF THE GOSPELS

In dealing with the books in the Old Testament which are still ascribed to Moses (The Pentateuch), David (The Psalms), and Solomon (Ecclesiastes), we are now familiar with the fact that the ascription of authorship to a biblical book does not necessarily imply personal authorship in our modern sense. Moses was the earliest law-giver, David "the sweet singer of Israel," Solomon the father of Wisdom: it therefore became an acknowledged principle to incorporate all subsequent laws under the name of Moses (including Deuteronomy which describes his death), all collections of sacred poetry under the name of David, and all Wisdom literature (which we might call philosophy; e.g. Ecclesiastes) under the name of Solomon.

The same sort of thing happened, though in rather a different way, with the four Gospels. As we shall see in the next chapter, these short accounts of the words and deeds of Jesus did not reach their present form until over thirty years after the Crucifixion. We know for certain that Mark and Luke were not members of the original apostolic band but joined the Christian fellowship after Pentecost, while the "Gospel According to Matthew" (which reproduces almost verbatim six hundred of Mark's six hundred and sixty-one verses) is quite obviously a compilation and is not the work of one single writer, while the Fourth Gospel (as we shall see in Chapter 14) cannot possibly come from the Apostle John, the son of Zebedee. These four little books seem to have been compiled to meet the natural demand of new converts to Christiantity who would know nothing of the earthly life of Jesus. (It is significant that St. Paul, whose letters are of an earlier date than the Gospels, never refers to any of the gospel stories or actual words of Jesus.) They appear to have been written in different places as well as at different times. Matthew, with its strongly marked Jewish colouring and its emphasis on Jesus as the Messiah, was evidently compiled by a Jewish Christian for converts from Judaism, and probably took its rise in Jerusalem, the first headquarters of the Church. Mark (as we shall see in Chapter

10) would have been written in Rome, under the direction of Peter. Luke is the work of the Greek physician who was the travelling companion of St. Paul, and may well have been written by him in Antioch, and this book was obviously written for non-Jews. John is a work of a totally different kind and takes the form more of a meditation than of a biography, and was almost certainly (as we shall see in Chapter 14) written in Ephesus.

What we call "editing" in the modern sense did not exist in the ancient world, neither did ancient writers ever acknowledge their sources. They do not appear to have had anything corresponding with our methods of sifting evidence or of winnowing out the wheat from the chaff of a traditional story, and they even sometimes placed side by side two quite inconsistent accounts of the same event.

These and other considerations which will crop up in the course of the chapters which follow should put the reader of the Gospels on his guard against anything like a *literal* acceptance of their testimony. We can believe that they are recording the actual words and deeds of Jesus, but we should never feel in any way bound to accept as true the *form* in which they present them. This was expressed authoritatively by the Doctrinal Commission (1938) of the Archbishops of Canterbury and York in the following words:

"Christian thinkers are not necessarily bound to the thought-forms employed by the Biblical writers . . .

. . . The authority ascribed to the Bible must not be interpreted as prejudging the conclusions of historical, critical, and scientific investigation in any field, not excluding that of the Biblical documents themselves." (*Doctrine in the Church of England*, p. 32)—S.P.C.K.

COUNTY OF DURHAM
NEVILLE'S CROSS
COLLEGE
EDUCATION COMMITTEE

Some Approximate Dates of New Testament Literature and Events

A.D.

29 or 30	The Crucifixion of Jesus.
32 or 34	The Conversion of St. Paul.
45	The Letter to the Galatians.
46	I and II Thessalonians.
52–54	I and II Corinthians.
58	The Letter to Romans.
60	Letters to Colossians, Philemon, Philippians and Ephesians.
64	Execution of St. Paul under Nero.
65 or 66	Gospel of Mark.
70	Destruction of Jerusalem by Titus.
78 or 85	Gospels of Matthew and Luke.
100–110	Gospel of John and John's Letters.

CHAPTER TEN

"Behold the Man!"

In our modern world it has become almost a matter of course for a well-known man to publish his autobiography or his private journal or diary. If he does not, someone is almost certain to write a book about him either during his lifetime or else within a short time of his death, and such books quite often become "best sellers."

In the ancient world we have nothing exactly corresponding to this type of literature. Plutarch's *Lives of the Noble Greeks and Romans* could hardly be called biographies in the modern sense. All they contain is a few personal reminiscences, some characteristic sayings and usually a disproportionately long account of the man's death.

Cicero, St. Paul and St. Augustine are perhaps the only men of the first five centuries of our era whom we can really claim to know, because their personal letters or *Confessions* (as in Augustine's case) have survived. In the case of Jesus of Nazareth we have nothing first hand. It would never have occurred to him to write his autobiography; and if he ever wrote any letters, none of them have survived. Stranger still it seems to us that no one appears to have written anything at all about him in the way of biography until nearly a generation after his death. There is, as we shall see presently, one completely sufficient reason for this.

But that does not mean that he was not the talk of the towns and villages of Palestine for years. We can be sure that so long as any were alive who had known him or had heard him or had been set on their feet by him, his name was a household word.

In a day when books were scarce, reminiscences were no doubt more fully and freely exchanged in conversation than is the case with us; so that when at long last the four gospels came to be written, there must have been a considerable amount of oral tradition upon which to draw. The more recent investigators into the origin of our written gospels are of the opinion that it is to this source that a good many of the sayings of Jesus and stories about him can be traced.

For the first thirty years or so after the Crucifixion, we know that those who had been most closely associated with the Master—his apostles—went about as travelling missionaries, telling people about him in all sorts of places and circumstances, in Jewish synagogues to congregations assembled for worship, in the open air to crowds in the market places or on hillsides, in chance encounters here, there, and everywhere.

It does not seem to have occurred to them or their earliest hearers to write anything down. Preachers and teachers may have made a few notes and jottings for their private use, but they do not seem to have felt any need to get anything transcribed in an ordered form. Even St. Paul, whose letters are actually the earliest Christian documents which have come down to us, does not quote any of the actual sayings of Jesus except one, "It is more blessed to give than to receive," which, strangely enough, does not appear in the four gospels. Neither does St. Paul refer in his letters to any of the incidents in the life of the Master beyond the bare facts of his birth, death and resurrection.

There is, however, one completely sufficient reason to account for this lack of early written material about the things which the historical Jesus said and did. From St. Paul's earliest letters, in particular the two letters to the Christian community at Thessalonica, it is clear that the early church confidently expected what we have come to call the "Second Advent." They expected that, *"this same Jesus which is taken up from you into heaven, shall so come in like manner as ye have seen him go into heaven"* (Acts 1: 11). This belief was so strongly held that St. Paul had to warn the Thessalonian Church, *"I beg you, brothers, not to let your minds get quickly unsettled or excited by any spirit of prophecy or any declaration or any letter purporting to come from me, to the effect that the Day of the Lord is already here."* When Christians parted from one another, instead of saying "Goodbye," they were in the habit of saying "Maranatha," which means "The Lord is near." This belief in the immediate literal personal return of Christ within their own lifetime was based on the highly poetic language current at the time in Jewish circles which Jesus himself may have used, contained in phrases like *"the Son of Man coming in the clouds of heaven."* There was a whole literature (known to us as Apocalyptic) which dwelt upon such expectations of some sort of supernatural "break through," which fortunately was never included in the Canon of Jewish Scripture but which was adopted by many of the early Christians (many of whom were devout Jews) and identified with the return of Christ. I will quote one specimen of such writings from a book called The Book of Enoch.

"And behold! He cometh with ten thousands of his holy ones to execute judgment upon all, and to destroy the ungodly; to convict all flesh of all the works of their ungodliness which they ungodly have committed, and of all the hard things which ungodly sinners have spoken against him."

If the historical Jesus did make use of this kind of apocalyptic language (some of which is to be found in St. Mark, Chapter 13), one cannot doubt that he used it poetically, and not literally, to convey the idea of the continued impact of his spirit and his teaching upon the ages. I believe it to be quite beyond the resources of scholarship ever to come to a definite conclusion upon these matters, which have been the subject of endless books and controversies now for the best part of a century. What is certain is that the belief in a second coming in their own lifetime was so strongly held by these early Christians that they did not think it worth while to write anything down for posterity. There was going to be no posterity to read it.

As the years went by, it gradually became clear to the best minds in the Church—and especially to the mind of St. Paul, as his language in his later letters shows—that they had been mistaken in allowing people to cling to a belief in a literal re-appearance of Christ on earth. A late sub-Apostolic letter (II Peter) quotes words which show that people were saying, *"Where is the promise of his coming? for from the day our fathers fell asleep, all things continue as they were from the beginning of the creation."* It was then, when new converts, most of them non-Jews, began to pour into the Churches, that the demand for knowledge of what the historic

Jesus had taught and done began to be answered by written records. A great many of these so-called "Gospels" were written, as the preface to St. Luke's Gospel declares: *"forasmuch as many have taken in hand to draw up a narrative concerning those matters which have been fulfilled amongst us."* More than twenty of these have survived. To name a few, we have "The Nativity of Mary," "The History of Joseph the Carpenter," "The Gospel of Thomas," "The Gospel of Nicodemus." A glance at some of these is enough to make us admire the wisdom of the Church in selecting Matthew, Mark, Luke and John as the four to be included in the Canon of Scripture. I will quote one passage from the Gospel of Thomas to show the crude and grotesque nature of most of these writings. Describing an incident in the boyhood of Jesus (of which we know nothing authentic beyond his visit to the Temple at the age of twelve) the author wrote:

"And Jesus took of the clay of the fish-pond and made of it twelve sparrows. And it was the sabbath day when Jesus did this. . . . And Joseph said 'Why hast thou done that which is not lawful on the sabbath?' And Jesus opened his hands and ordered the clay sparrows saying, 'Go up into the air and fly: nobody will kill you.' And they flew and began to cry out and praise God Almighty."

Anyone who has ever read a page or two of our four Gospels can see that they stand on a totally different level from that, though, as we shall see later, even some of *them* (especially St. Matthew) show a strong tendency to depreciate the humanity of Jesus by heightening the miraculous and by suggesting that his knowledge and powers during his earthly life were not subject to our limitations. Ever since the scientific study of the New Testament began, there have been widely different views and attitudes towards what is called "the miraculous element" in the Gospels, and any discussion of them would take us far beyond the scope of this book. Suffice it to say with Mr. W. E. H. Lecky, the historian, that the age in which Jesus and the apostles lived was "predisposed towards the miraculous"; that is to say, the climate of thought was favourable to the belief in miracles just as our climate of thought is unfavourable. While we, I think quite rightly, would exhaust every possible natural explanation of an event before accepting a supernatural explanation, they would never bother about investigating natural causes at all. That, of course, is true of the whole Bible. The idea of what we call "natural laws" was not born till the Rennaissance and the beginning of the scientific age. People in those days believed that God acted directly on things and events in the material world: it was only the great prophets who had come to realise that God only acts in the world of men through the *minds* of men. Jesus stands in the succession of those great prophets, and that goes far to explain his obvious dislike of being asked to give "A Sign from Heaven." This is so important that I shall quote here from what I should take as the finest modern commentary on the Gospels, "The Mission and Message of Jesus":

> "The attitude of Jesus towards miracles differed from that of his contemporaries and followers. In our earliest Gospel sources, Jesus condemns the faith in him which rests on miracles. He declares that it is an evil and adulterous generation which seeks after a sign: in other words, a generation unfaithful to God which demands signs and wonders as the basis for its religious faith. . . . He asserted that if men would not hear Moses and the prophets, neither would they be persuaded though one rose from the dead." (Major, Manson and Wright. *The Mission and Message of Jesus*, p. 27.)

No one who has set his mind free from a literal acceptance of the words of Scripture should feel any difficulty, therefore, in being unable to accept the explanation or lack of explanation of certain events as they are recorded in the narratives of the four Gospels. Even the modern journalist who professes to give us facts cannot "write them up" without colouring them to some extent with his own personal interpretation. There is no such thing as a "bald fact" if it belongs to past history, for the simple reason that it can only reach us through the human mind—our own or some-one else's—which has apprehended it. All the greater, then, is our justification, in reading these ancient Gospels, for making due allowances for the climate of opinion of the age and the personal idiosyncrasies of the writers, none of whom were actually eye-witnesses of the events or actually hearers of the words which they have recorded. That is not so much a disadvantage as might at first sight appear. Archbishop William Temple made it very clear when he wrote, "It is the uncertainty about every detail of the Gospel Record which finally secures its purely spiritual authority. Its general outline and its main facts—such as the Crucifixion—are assured. But if there were one detailed thing of which we could be absolutely sure and say there can be no doubt whatever that He did this or said that, no doubt of any kind, *that* would immediately be a binding fact, a hard nugget, so to speak, of imposed conviction which we should have to accept even though our spirits made no response to it." (*Daily Readings from William Temple*, 1068. Ed. H. C. Warner. Hodder & Stoughton.)

What I wish to do, then, in the remainder of this chapter is to make a few suggestions as to how, by reading the earliest of the four gospels, *According to St. Mark*, we can come into touch spiritually with the Man of Nazareth.

As I have already said, none of the Four Gospels actually come from eyewitnesses; but the Gospel of Mark is the nearest approach to this. It may contain some of the reminiscences of Simon Peter. If this can be substantiated, as I believe it can, the Gospel of Mark can bring us closer to the historical Jesus than any of the others.

At this point it is of the first importance that you should use a modern translation. (James Moffat: *The New Testament, a new Translation*, is probably the best.) The Authorised Version with its verse divisions makes it far more difficult to get any vivid impression of the personality of Jesus, and that is what we need to counteract the terribly unreal associations which have been built up in most people's minds by stained glass windows, children's picture-books and the like. It is impossible to over-estimate the harm that is still being done by these misrepresentations, for in them we are always being shown either a Kingly figure complete with crown and sceptre or a feeble attenuated creature with no suggestion of the vigorous health and strength Christ must have possessed. It is good to see that some of the popular pictures by artists like Harold Copping are now getting into our schools, for these are bringing back into the minds of children something of the young carpenter of Nazareth, the eldest son of a working man's family, the friend and companion of the men of the Galilean lake and the fishmarket, the man whose robust sense of humour could penetrate the defences of pious humbug and whose flashing eye could beckon men to a great adventure. That is one's impression of him from the first three chapters of this gospel of Mark.

Let us look at them in a little more detail. What is the picture? Something of this sort. Steady matter-of-fact men settled in a well-established business find the habits of a lifetime suddenly disturbed, broken up and changed. *"Come, follow me,"* says Jesus, *"and I will make you fish for men"* (1 : 17). They leave all, and go with him. A sabbath congregation that had gathered week in and week out for years in the local synagogue to yawn through the solemn discourses of dry-as-dust Rabbis are suddenly electrified: *"It's new teaching with authority behind it!"* they exclaim. Invalids who have given up hope, believing themselves to be under the wrath and punishment of God, are told that their sins are not only forgiven but forgotten: they are released into a new life and told that it is their own faith, not his power, that has cured them. Fussy pedantic sabbatarians who by imposing pettifogging little rules and regulations had turned what had been originally intended as "a day of rest" into an inhuman burden, have the ground cut from under their feet by one sharp pointed sentence—*"The Sabbath was made for man, not man for the Sabbath."* The "good and godly ones" coming out of church on another bright Sabbath morning observe him and his fishermen friends deliberately breaking the Sabbath laws by rubbing in their hands the ears of corn which they have plucked as they walked through the cornfields. When reproved by the Pharisees (who formed the inner circle of Church life) he simply reminds them of the episode of King David taking his hungry soldiers into the "house of God" and eating "the loaves of the Presence" which no layman was allowed to touch. Human needs must come before Church regulations. A breath of fresh air blows through the stuffiness of religious conventionality when he begs leave to be excused from

observing an official Fast (like our Lent) because he and his disciples are like a wedding party and can therefore hardly be expected to don the sackcloth and ashes. He has come to life as to a
marriage feast. Churchiness, snobbery and exclusiveness go down
before his open association and friendship with persons generally
considered to be beyond the pale, and he whose eagle eye can
always catch the glitter of a rough diamond is content to remind
those who had lived sheltered lives that, after all, it is the sick who
need the doctor, not the whole. His is a practical religion of
sanctified common sense.

Then, if we look still closer, our eyes will be arrested by
interesting circumstantial details (not to be found in the other
Gospels) which bring vividness to the picture. The fisherman "left
their father Zebedaeus in the boat *with the crew*." "The whole
town was gathered *at the door*" (obviously of Jesus' home) (1: 33).
He got up *"long before daylight"* to go into the hills to pray (1: 35).
He would not let the healing ministry interfere with his main
work, which was preaching: *"Everybody is looking for you,"* said
Simon and his friends, but he said to them, *"Let us go somewhere
else to the adjoining country-towns, so that I may preach there as well:
that is why I came out here"* (1: 38). He needed quiet to prepare his
message. But most vivid of all in this first chapter is the ending
where Jesus, having been in contact with a leper, was evidently
regarded as "unclean" himself. The result was that Jesus *"could no
longer enter any town openly"* but *"He stayed outside in lonely places."*
So the healer found himself in quarantine.

The reports Mark gives of the impression on the crowds, and
the attitude of his family, are equally vivid and very strongly
suggest that they come from an eyewitness. After the healing of
the paralytic, the bystanders exclaimed, *"We never saw the like of
it!"* (2: 12). So great was the pressure of his work upon him that
"it was impossible even to have a meal." This led to trouble at home.
His family objected to his irregular habits: *"And when his family
heard this, they set out to get hold of him, for men were saying, 'He's out
of his mind'."* There is enough here and in the sixth chapter, where
Jesus remarked that a prophet *"is not without honour, except in his
native place and among his kinsfolk and in his home,"* to shatter all

the sentimental pictures of "the Holy Family." His was a very ordinary family, and Jesus knew as much if not more than most people about the tensions and misunderstandings which arise around the member who feels the claims of the larger family of God. St. Mark paints a graphic little picture, at the end of the third chapter, of the embarrassing situation which arose out of this.

> "*Then came his brothers and his mother, and standing outside they sent to call him; there was a crowd sitting round him, and he was told, 'Here are your mother and brothers and sisters wanting you outside.' He replied, 'Who are my mother and my brothers?' and glancing at those who were sitting round him in a circle he said, 'There are my mother and my brothers! Whoever does the will of God, that is my brother and sister and mother'.*"

Mark gives nothing more than a brief summary of his earliest teaching (1 : 14):

> "*The time has come at last—the Kingdom of God has arrived. You must change your hearts and minds and believe the good news.*" (J. B. Phillips' Translation.)

Expanded a little, it amounts to this: "I bring you a new thought of God. Spiritual power is available to you; unseen forces are playing upon your lives all the time and God is very near. You cannot live the full life of man unless you learn to tap the hidden resources of patience, courage and hope just above your heads but not beyond your reach. Cast out for ever from your minds all fear, all ideas of God as arbitrary, hard or inhuman, and learn to know him as I do, as the great Father who is waiting for you to come to him as his child."

The fourth chapter introduces us to the teaching method of Jesus through the parable of the Sower, which concludes with the characteristic words, "*Anyone who has ears to hear, let him listen to this*" (4 : 9).

Here again Mark sets the scene vividly. A vast crowd, "greater than ever," has followed Jesus down to the water's edge. He knows the difficulties of open-air speaking without a platform, and as the crowd surges so close that people at the back can neither see nor hear, he borrows Peter's boat and puts a little strip of water between himself and his audience in order that his resonant voice shall reach the farthest edge of the crowd. As we listen to this profound parable we find that we are all there in the multitude that has heard it down the ages, for human nature does not change. There is still the listener with the closed mind, beaten hard like the path around the field by the frequent passage of trivial thoughts; there is still the listener with the shallow sermon-tasting mind; and all the others. Jesus knew men's minds and hearts, and he knew his way into them.

But Mark hurries us on, for his object is not primarily to record teaching but to show us the Man. Next we have the storm on the lake. Here is a case in which we need to distinguish clearly between the facts and Mark's and the fishermen's interpretation of them. These people believed that storms were caused by demons (which also caused diseases). "The whole universe," says Dr. T. R. Glover, "was full of demon powers more real than the men and women in the streets." Therefore it is not at all surprising that when Jesus said, *"Peace, be quiet"* (4 : 39) the fishermen took it that he was addressing the storm demons, whereas no doubt he was really trying to calm their fears. "May we not assume that the wonder-story grew out of a remarkable coincidence. The rebuke administered by Jesus to a voluble and cowardly disciple, coinciding as it did with the subsidence of the storm, was interpreted by his wonder-loving disciples as a rebuke to the storm itself." (Major, Manson and Wright.)

In the days when belief in Christ as the revealer of God was thought to depend upon the literal acceptance of every word that these ancient writers said about him, all these wonder stories helped and confirmed the faith. Today, with our knowledge of their primitive beliefs which made these descriptions inevitable, they cannot be anything but a hindrance and a barrier to the living faith proclaimed by St. John that the works that He did we shall do also. It was natural that a later writer like Matthew, who actually reproduces in his own way six hundred of Mark's six hundred sixty-one verses and who compiled his gospel at a time when Jesus had become the centre of Christian devotion, should heighten the miraculous and so widen the gap between the prophet of Nazareth and ourselves. A careful reading of St. Mark narrows that gap. He gives us in one or two significant passages a picture of Jesus the healer working within the limitations with which spiritual healing today is making us familiar. In the sixth chapter we have an account of a visit of Jesus to his native place, Nazareth.

Here, we are told, familiarity bred contempt. His power was questioned. Was he not *"the joiner, the son of Mary and the brother of James and Joses and Judas and Simon? Are not his sisters settled here among us?"* The result was, says Mark, that *"HE COULD NOT DO ANY MIRACLE beyond laying his hands on a few sick people and curing them"*; and he adds, *"He was astonished at their lack of faith."* In reproducing this, Matthew omits the two vital words *"COULD NOT"* and simply says, *"he did not do there many miracles."*

Again in Chapter 8 there is another story which Mark alone records, of a gradual cure of blindness. After the first treatment the man is asked, *"Do you see anything?"* and replies, *"I can make out people, for I see them as large as trees moving."* Then Jesus again *"laid his hands on his eyes,"* and this time *"the man stared in front of him; he was quite restored, he saw everything plainly."*

From all this and much more that you may find for yourself in this earliest of the Gospels, it seems clear that the tradition about Mark's Gospel preserved by the historian Eusebius is authentic. He records the words of Papias, Bishop of Hierapolis about A.D. 125, "Mark, having become the interpreter of Peter, wrote down accurately everything he remembered, without, however, recording in order what was either said or done by Christ."

But who was this man Mark? I think there can be little room for doubt that he was the *"John whose surname was Mark"* of whom we hear later in the Acts of the Apostles and possibly in the first letter of Peter, who refers to "Mark, my son" (I Peter 5: 13). We know also from the Acts of the Apostles (12) that it was to the *"house of Mary, the mother of John whose surname was Mark,"* in Jerusalem that Peter went after escaping from prison. Putting these facts together we cannot be far wrong in indentifying the writer of this gospel with "*the young man*" of whom he speaks (Mark 14: 50-51), who had followed the disciples from the Upper Room (of the Last Supper) across the brook Kedron into the Garden of Gethsemane on the night of the betrayal. Mark, then, would be the son of the innkeeper who put the "Upper Room" at the disposal of Jesus on that momentous night. It is easy to picture the scene. No doubt his father had told the boy that the Teacher from Galilee was to arrive at dusk and that they were not to be disturbed. The night wears on and young Mark is supposed to have gone to bed. Presently he hears their voices rising into a hymn of praise, then their footsteps descending the stairs. Where are they going now, this mysterious party? Mark does not wait to dress; he winds a sheet around him and stealthily tiptoes out into the street after the retreating figures. They cross the brook to the foot of the Hill of Olives where there is a garden. Mark waits among the trees. Hours pass. Then in the midnight he sees the flare of torches and the gleam of spears and bright helmets. There is a scuffle and swords flash in the moonlight. Somebody grabs hold of him but he escapes leaving his sheet behind him. St. Mark 14: 50–51 reads:

"*Then the disciples left him and fled, all of them; one young man did follow him with only a linen sheet thrown round his body, but when the other youths seized him, he fled away naked, leaving the sheet behind him.*"

That little sentence which interrupts the narrative of the Agony in the Garden and appears in none of the other gospels is quite unnecessary unless it is the artist's signature in the corner of his picture, the earliest picture of the Man of Nazareth.

CHAPTER ELEVEN

According to Matthew

THE story goes that an elderly lady who had been brought up to accept everything in the Bible quite literally put down her New Testament with the remark, "How dreadful! According to that, Jesus must have been crucified four times!" Her rather naïve difficulty might have been resolved at once if she had given full value to the two words at the head of each of the four gospels— "*According to . . .*" These two words can only mean that we are reading here four different versions of the same story. It would therefore be unreasonable (unless we start off with the idea that every word of the Bible is literally true) to expect four different accounts of the deeds and words of Jesus to agree with one another either in general presentation or in particular details.

As we have seen in the previous chapter, our four gospels were selected by the Church from a much larger number as the most authentic. But the words *According to* should be a sufficient warning to even the most literal-minded reader neither to expect complete agreement nor to accept these documents as infallibly and finally true, especially where the personal idiosyncrasies of the different writers are at all pronounced. In reading the Gospels, or any other Biblical writings, one should have in mind St. Paul's guiding principle, "*The letter killeth, but the Spirit giveth Life.*"

In any case, Matthew Arnold's warning that Jesus is always above the heads of his reporters applies to the four gospels just as much as to the countless "Lives of Christ" which have appeared since. The personality of Jesus Christ is so great and many-sided that it is little wonder that everybody sees in him just that particular feature which appeals most to himself. If he ventures to write a "Life of Christ," he cannot help allowing his personal convictions or even his personal prejudices (which are nearly always unconscious) from colouring his book. "It is easy," says Dr. Raven in his recent Gifford Lectures, "to collect a number of books recently written in which Jesus is despicted as a pacifist or a die-hard, a dreamer, a Rotarian, a social-reformer, a mystic or an apocalyptist . . . one or two represent him as a Communist and his Church as a world-revolutionary movement."

Now this very natural human tendency to emphasise and isolate one particular aspect of his personality must be clearly recognised by the reader of the "Gospel according to St. Matthew." If it is not, then I am afraid that our general impression would be that the whole life of Jesus on this earth was pre-determined and stage-managed from heaven in order to give literal fulfilment to certain words of Isaiah or one of the other Old Testament prophets. With monotonous reiteration the writer of this book tells us again and again that this or that took place in the life of Jesus *that it might be fulfilled which was spoken by the prophet.* In nearly every case the reference is quite artificial and unwarranted, especially those which Matthew quotes to try and prove to his Jewish or Jewish Christian readers that Jesus was the Messiah. In the first two chapters, the birth of Jesus at Bethlehem, the return from Egypt and the massacre of the Innocents are all said to be literal fulfilments of words arbitrarily selected from Micah, Hosea and Jeremiah respectively, which related to events in past history or events contemporary, with those prophets. The most notable of these, of course, is the sentence from Isaiah 7: 14 which Matthew has adopted as a prophecy of the Virgin Birth.

"Behold, a virgin shall conceive and bear a son, and shall call his name Immanuel."

Anyone who reads the words in their original context can see at once that Isaiah was speaking of a child likely to be born within a few weeks or months, whose mother would be so elated at the change in the nation's fortunes that she would call him "Immanuel," which means "God is with us." Jerusalem was threatened at that time with a formidable coalition of the Syrians and the Ephraemites which would in all probability end in a siege of some months. Isaiah, accompanied by his son, Shearjashub (another optimistic name meaning "A-remnant-shall-return") meets King Ahaz just as he is inspecting the city's water supply. The prophet calms the King's fears by telling him that within a few months the danger will be all over. "If you want a sign or omen of this," he says, "a young expectant mother (very likely there in the crowd) will shortly give birth to a son whom she will be able to call Immanuel (God-is-with-us), for before her child is weaned, and certainly before he knows good from evil, the dangerous coalition will have broken up." There is a double error here in applying this to the birth of Jesus. Not only had Isaiah's words nothing to do with any child except one to be born within the next few months of his speaking them, but the original Hebrew word in Isaiah does not mean "virgin" but simply "young woman" (Hebrew HALMA). If Isaiah had wished to say "virgin" he would have used the proper Hebrew word for it which is BETHULAH. To add to the complication Matthew, like all New Testament writers, was quoting from the Greek Version of the Old Testament (The Septuagint) which for some unknown reason mistranslated the Hebrew HALMA (young woman) by the Greek word PARTHENOS which means "Virgin." I am glad to see that the American standard Revised Bible has corrected the error in the English text of "Isaiah" by printing "young woman" and not "virgin."

There is no space here for further discussion of the doctrine of the Virgin Birth, which has been very largely built upon this passage and which has assumed so prominent a position in the theology of the Christian Church. Suffice it to say that in both the Gospels (Matthew and Luke) which contain the story (and contain it in very different versions) there is placed beside it a genealogical tree showing Our Lord's descent through Joseph. Whatever the value of these family trees as authentic documents may or may not be, they point very definitely to the fact that there existed from the earliest times the opposite tradition of the birth of Jesus through the ordinary processes of human generation. And there is a good deal more evidence in the Gospel of Luke, which speaks of "his parents," to substantiate this. In this case as in others, if only the habit common to Biblical writers of putting into their books two contradictory traditions side by side had been more frankly recognised, a great deal of unnecessary controversy would have been avoided. Both views of our Lord's birth can claim to be "Scriptural" and therefore (as the Doctrinal Commission of 1938 makes it clear) those of us who find the non-miraculous tradition more in keeping with a belief in our Lord's true manhood are just as orthodox as those who cherish the Virgin Birth tradition. In any case we can hold a belief in Christ's unique consciousness of sonship or divinity on grounds which seemed sufficient to the author of the Fourth Gospel—who has no "birth-stories" in his book at all.

But Matthew's handling (or rather mishandling) of the Old Testament is not the only thing that gives the modern reader the impression of unreality. So anxious is this writer to stress the divinity of Jesus that he frequently heightens the miraculous and so tends to obscure the natural human limitations within which (according to Mark, the earlier gospel) Jesus worked. Besides the instance given in the previous chapter where Mark's statement that Jesus COULD NOT do any mighty work in Nazareth is changed by Matthew into DID NOT, we have the still more significant alteration in the story of the young man who came and said to Jesus, "Good Master, what shall I do to inherit eternal life?" and Jesus said to him, *"Why callest thou me good? None is good save one, even God"* (Mark 10 : 17–18). Matthew changes Jesus' answer to, *"Why askest thou me concerning that which is good?"* Such a change is quite deliberate on the part of this writer. He obviously thought that it was just as improper to allow Jesus to refuse to be called "good" as it would be to suggest that he could not perform his cures without the co-operative faith of his patients. There are several other instances of this.

Then there is the strange story of the cursing of the fig tree. In Mark's account, Jesus and his disciples are walking from Bethany to Jerusalem. On the way Jesus is disappointed at finding no fruit on a fig tree, *"for it was not the season of figs."* In thoroughly Eastern fashion he says, *"No man eat fruit from thee henceforward for ever!"* Mark adds that the disciples heard it. They spend the day in Jerusalem, during which Jesus clears the Temple of the hucksters of sacrificial victims and returns to Bethany for the night. Next morning, walking up the same road, the disciples draw his attention to the fig tree which he had "cursed," pointing out that it has withered away. A sharp frost and a hot sun would be quite enough to account for this. But Matthew turns it into an instantaneous miracle (and a most unedifying one at that) by reporting that the moment Jesus had uttered the curse *"immediately the fig tree withered away."*

But quite the most far-fetched stories which Matthew, and Matthew alone, has given us are connected with the Crucifixion and the Resurrection. At the Crucifixion, *"Rocks were split and tombs were opened, and a number of bodies of the saints . . . rose up . . . and appeared to a number of people."* At the resurrection an angel descended from heaven, *"rolled away the stone from the sepulchre and sat upon it; and his appearance was like lightning and his raiment white as snow, and for fear of him the watchers did quake and became as dead men."* According to all the other writers the manifestations of the Risen Lord were given privately and personally to confirm the faith of his disciples. One can detect in Matthew's story that crude supernatural note of popular Messianic expectation which is utterly alien to all that we know of the Spirit of Jesus and the ways of God with men. In reading any of the stories of the Resurrection we should study the spiritual experiences of the disciples rather than descriptions of phenomena. All words are inadequate symbols of thought, especially those which attempt to convey one's spiritual experiences. And we have only the language of the five senses at our disposal.

I have drawn the reader's attention in some detail to these very obvious faults in this Gospel of Matthew partly to illustrate the lengths to which a writer's presuppositions may carry him, and also to throw into bolder relief the greatness of the contribution which Matthew's Gospel has made to our knowledge of Jesus as the true interpreter and fulfiller of the law and the Prophets. It is a striking fact that there is all the difference in the world between the way in which Matthew treats the Old Testament and the way in which he describes Jesus as having treated it. In fact, so great is the contrast that we should be fully justified on this ground alone in not attributing the Gospel of Matthew to a single writer. It is much more likely to have been the work of an editor incorporating materials from several different sources besides the Gospel of

Mark. And this is now the general opinion of New Testament scholars. Both in his account of Our Lord's Temptation (Matthew 4), and in his record of the Sermon on the Mount (Matthew 5, 6, 7), Matthew shows that certain books of the Old Testament, especially Deuteronomy, Isaiah and The Book of Psalms, were among the chief formative influences of the mind of Jesus. Let us look at both of these passages in some detail because, as I have said, they form between them Matthew's greatest contribution to our knowledge of Jesus both as a student and as a teacher.

It is quite clear that by the age of thirty (and we have no reliable information about Jesus until that age) Jesus had got a great deal of the literature both of the Psalmists and the Prophets by heart, as well as certain key passages in Deuteronomy (which was the very latest revision of the Mosaic Law). Now it is one thing to know a passage by heart, as every child of the Jewish synagogue did, but quite another thing to have so digested and absorbed it that it has become part of the very stuff of one's mind. This is what had been happening to Jesus from boyhood. It first becomes apparent when Jesus accepted baptism at the hands of his cousin, John the Baptist. John was definitely a representative of the Apocalyptic school. His preaching was of the hell-fire type with which we have been made woefully familiar throughout the Christian centuries, which draws a sharp distinction between "the righteous" and "sinners." In it, whenever it appears, is the idea that God is favourable to the one and hostile to the other. When the penitents arrive at the Jordan to be baptised they are greeted with, "*Who hath warned you to flee from the wrath to come?*"

Jesus arrives at the Jordan and accepts John's baptism but certainly not his message of God's hostility to sinners. The experience of Jesus as he came up from the Jordan was of a totally different kind. In direct contrast to John's thunderous denunciations, Jesus experiences in the depths of his being something unspeakably calm and quiet and gentle which is symbolised by a dove's alighting. For him, as for John, the veil between the seen and the unseen is "rent asunder"; but the God who speaks, speaks in the tones which Hosea and Second Isaiah had heard, tones of infinite loving-kindness and tender mercy.

"Thou art my son, the beloved, in thee is my delight."

The words "Thou art my son" are a quotation from Psalm 2; "the beloved, in thee is my delight" comes from Isaiah 42. This shows us very clearly how Jesus selected the great spiritual ideas of different Old Testament writers and combined them together in his mind and pondered them until they had become the authentic voice of God speaking to him. If he had gone on quoting Psalm 2, he would have come upon words alien to his whole outlook, for the Psalmist goes on to describe this "son" or "Messiah," as "ruling the Nations with a rod of iron and breaking them in pieces like a potter's vessel." So he turns in his mind to what he had come to believe to be the true function of the son or servant of God, described by Isaiah, who would not "break the broken reed or quench the smoking flax" (Isa. 42).

So the Gospel of Matthew makes it clear from the start, by presenting us with this account of Jesus' first spiritual experience, that he had already broken—and broken completely—with traditional ideas about God and his relationship with men, particularly with sinners. His was to be a real "Gospel" or piece of Good News about the love of God towards sinners. In direct contrast with the whole attitude of the school of John the Baptist, we soon hear the gracious invitation, *"Come unto me, all ye that labour and are heavy laden, and I will give you rest."* (Matt. 11: 28). It is most striking that Jesus issued that invitation immediately after speaking words in which he claimed to know God as a son knows his father's innermost mind. *"No one knoweth the Father save the Son, and he to whomsoever the Son willeth to reveal him."* In a word, Jesus said that we cannot find our way to a vital knowledge of God except through realising, as he had, the filial relationship in which we all stand to Our Father who is in heaven.

The narrative of the Temptation, in which we see again how Jesus derives his inspiration from the Old Testament, shows clearly that his method of making God known to men will be consistent with the experience through which he had come to know God himself. In the brief compass of eleven verses, Matthew describes in what we should call poetic prose the tremendous spiritual experience through which Jesus must have passed, an experience which determined his whole future career. At the back of his mind was the conviction that the filial relationship which he had found with God was to be for all mankind. But the problem for him was how people were to be brought into it. Where was he to begin? He knew well enough where his fellow countrymen would like him to begin. What they wanted was a better standard of living all round. Palestine was an occupied country, times were hard, taxation was crippling, food was scarce. What was the use of talking about spiritual things to men with empty stomachs? Would not the first step be to improve the economic conditions of the country? This is all contained in the picturesque phrase, "turning stones into bread." But as Jesus entertained that thought and pictured to himself the well-fed prosperous community which he would dearly like to see, one great sentence from the book of Deuteronomy led him to reject it. *"Man shall not live by bread alone, but by every word that proceedeth out of the mouth of God."* In a word, he realised that you will never bring people into a new and fuller life and a more vital relationship with God simply by improving their material conditions. Things must be changed from the inside first.

A more vital relationship with God—that is what we needed. Then why not try to solve the problem from the spiritual end? Could he not get God to break through by some dramatic demonstration of supernatural power such as the popular religious literature of the day (apocalyptic) was always declaring? This thought is vividly presented in the phrase about casting himself down from one of the pinnacles of Herod's temple which he could probably see glittering in the sunlight as he looked across the desert. Jesus weighed up that idea too in the light of some words he remembered from Psalm 91 which seemed at first to give him good scriptural warrant for accepting it.

"He shall give his angels charge concerning thee, and in their hands they shall bear thee up lest at any time thou dash thy foot against a stone."

Would not a miracle bring the crowds to his feet, and would not a career as a wonder-working magician pave the way for his work as a teacher? Would not the good end which he sought more than justify the rather questionable means which he was sorely tempted to employ? In long sleepless nights he must have wrestled with this until he saw it at length as a temptation of the devil. Could it possibly be right to apply material tests to spiritual power and to expect divine interventions in answer to prayer? Once again the book of Deuteronomy reminded him, "*Thou shalt not tempt* (or test) *the Lord thy God.*" This rejection of the miraculous as a means of bringing people to God is fundamental to our understanding of his "mighty works" of healing of which we read in all the gospels. It was this decision to heal the sick and to reinstate sinners *within the limits of their faith,* and in no other way, which marks Jesus out as the true revealer of the God who is not the great Magician but the good Physician of men and nations.

Having rejected those two extreme methods, a third which seemed to come somewhere in between them presented itself to his mind. Why not respond to the most popular demand of all and assume the role of the Warrior Messiah whose "dominion shall be from one sea to another and from the flood unto the world's end"? Alexander the Great's conquest of the whole known world three hundred years before had brought so good and beneficial a thing as Greek culture to the peoples of the Mediterranean world. How much more he could do for mankind than Alexander! But once again there was this question of the means by which he was to gain control of the "nations of the world" for God. There was no way so far devised by the wit of man but force, which Jesus came to see for the blasphemous thing it is, devil-worship.

Here is the relevance of the Bible for today. There is no other way to bring men to God but the way which Jesus chose when he had rejected both materialism, magic (propaganda) and the use of force—and that is the way of love. He decided there and then to make his appeal to the heart of mankind by a method which mankind has never yet tried on a universal scale, the method not of dictatorship but of service, the method not of domination but of suffering and sacrifice. Jesus went out into the wilderness knowing that he was the Son of the Most High (the constant repetition, *"If thou be the Son of God,"* makes us sure of that): he came back into Galilee knowing that he was the Servant of the lowliest, the least, and the lost. He must serve not as some of the prophets had foretold, with a mighty hand and a stretched-out arm, but as the Second Isaiah had seen, with the wounded hand of that servant who should at long last *"see the travail of his soul and be satisfied."*

At this point the reader may feel that I have forgotten the purpose of this book, which is simply to draw attention to some of the main features of the Bible, and toss it impatiently aside. I don't mind very much if he does, provided that he then takes up the Gospel of Matthew instead and reads *at a sitting* the next three chapters—the fifth, sixth and seventh. For here is the greatest feature of all, the longest piece of connected teaching which has come down to us from Jesus Christ, the "Sermon on the Mount."

In conversation the other day with an otherwise reasonably educated citizen, I mentioned "The Sermon on the Mount." "The Sermon on the Mount?" she said. "What is that?" Well, to begin with, I think that the title we have given to this supremely great piece of teaching is misleading. I was taught that a sermon should be like a pencil; it should have one point and that a sharp one! But the Sermon on the Mount, which I have just read through in twelve minutes, is quite unlike any sermon I have ever heard. I feel much more as if I had been reading a poem which I shall want to read every so often for the rest of my life. Perhaps it would be better to call it, "The Spring-Song of the New World." That might prevent literal-minded people from taking a verse here and a verse there and quoting it in isolation as though it were a law. Jesus was not a law-giver but a poet. That is the first thing to be realised. Pick out some of these sentences and try to apply them literally and you will either have to dismiss them as unpractical idealism unrelated to life in this world, or else you will impose upon your conscience a strain which you were never meant to endure.

For example:

> "*Give to him that asketh of thee, and from him that would borrow of thee, turn not thou away.*"

Taken literally, that means indiscriminate charity.

> "*Resist not evil.*"

Taken literally, that means absolute pacifism, as does also

> "*Whosoever smiteth thee on the right cheek, turn to him the other also.*"

In the same way, just picture the scene in your parish church if, just before the Offertory, everybody, including the minister, got up and walked out of the church. Yet that is what we should all want to do if we took Matthew 5:23 literally:

> "*So if you are offering your gift at the altar and there remember that your brother has something against you, leave your gift there before the altar and go away; first be reconciled to your brother, and then come and offer your gift.*"

A great deal of unnecessary controversy would have been avoided if only people would recognise that the sayings of Jesus in the Sermon on the Mount (and elsewhere) about divorce, for instance, are not absolute laws forbidding it under all circumstances but simply broad general statements of the *ideal* of a life-long indissoluble relationship. Ideals are like the highest mountains: not everyone can climb them and no penalty (as in the case of law) should be imposed upon those who fail. In this matter English law is more merciful and nearer to the mind of Christ than some rigorist spokesmen of the Anglican Church. In the Sermon on the Mount, Jesus is enunciating the ideal principles on which we are to try and live as sons and daughters of the Most High. So in the sayings we have quoted he is commending to us the general principles of generosity ("Give"), non-violence ("Resist not"). acceptance as opposed to retaliation ("Turn the other cheek"), and reconciliation with one's fellow men as more important than making offerings to the Church. In short, Jesus is telling us to re-examine our scale of values and to put first things first.

"Seek ye first the Kingdom of God."

That this was his object is made very clear by the words, *"so that ye may be sons of your Father who is in heaven: for he makes his sun rise on the evil and the good, and sends rain on the just and the unjust."*

It's no good whatever asking people to behave in this magnanimous way, even to the extent of loving one's enemies and doing good to those who do one evil, unless they are sure that they've got enough of their Father in them to be equal to the challenge and to "overcome evil with good." The whole of this teaching in the Sermon on the Mount rests upon that consciousness of sonship. It is not theoretical; it is the practical consequence and the only logical consequence of having accepted, as Jesus had, the fact of sonship with God. *"If thou art the son of God"*—this is the only way to live the good life, something miles beyond obedience to man-made laws, which have to be for the most part negative.

Legal systems, like the Ten Commandments, are of course necessary and always will be, simply because in every generation people are at vastly varying stages of moral and intellectual development. Our primary instincts cannot be allowed free rein. They must be restrained by prohibitive laws, if society is to be saved from barbarism and anarchy. But, says Jesus, you will never progress towards a better state of society simply by restraining and punishing the wrong-doer; neither will progress come through people who can claim nothing more than that they have kept all the commandments from their youth up. I recall an old man who told me that he'd lived a good life and had nothing to regret. When I said that personally I had a good deal to regret already, he replied by bringing out what he thought was his trump-card—"Never been to jail once!" It was too late to try and shatter his complacence!

If mankind is to "rise on stepping stones of its dead self to higher things," it is necessary that "our righteousness," our standard, should be much higher than that required by any law. If we are to be pioneers and creators of a new and better world, we shall have to be new men and women ourselves. If we are to be at all like Christ himself, we shall have to learn as he did to resolve our inner conflicts. That is the meaning of his exacting words: "It was said to them of old time, 'No Murder'; I say, 'No Anger'." "It was said to them of old time, 'No Adultery'; I say 'No Lust'." "It was said to them of old time, 'No Perjury'; I say 'No Insincerity'." "But let your 'Yea' be 'Yea,' and your 'Nay' be 'Nay'." We are not to wait for the law to step in and restrain evil; we are to nip evil in the bud by imposing a stricter discipline on our thoughts, or, in more popular language, by learning to consume our own smoke.

Thus gradually we shall become really free, integrated, happy people such as Jesus describes in the Beatitudes (Matthew 5: 1–11). Let me try to summarise them. To be "poor in spirit" doesn't mean to be poor-spirited, but to have a divine discontent with one's spiritual progress. To be a "mourner" doesn't mean to wear black and be miserable; it means to have woken up to the fact that this life is not all and to find strength and comfort in that thought. To be "meek" doesn't mean to be unable to say boo to a goose; it means to accept everything that life brings without complaining and without claiming anything as one's right. To be truly "meek" is to possess the freedom of the earth just as a distinguished man is given the "freedom of the city." Goodness is never goody-goodiness or spiritual snobbishness: it is magnanimity, that true greatness which is free from self-pity or self-praise and in which "the "quality of mercy is not strained." To be a "peacemaker" does not consist in sticking a badge on your chest or attending Peace Meetings; it is to be strong enough to carry all the taunts and unjust accusations, all the evil which may be done to you, and just let it all thaw in the flame of the love of God which Jesus calls "*the light which is in you.*" That, he says, is the truly happy or "blessed" life. Happiness will not come to you if you pursue it as the be-all and end-all of life, for it is not a product so much as a by-product, a consequence of trying to live as a son of God. The word "blessed" is better than "happy" because it is associated with those who have passed beyond physical death. We speak of them somtimes as "the blessed." That suggests that the Christian disciple is really one who is trying to establish the conditions of the "after life" here in the present work-a-day world. Would not that be the best answer to those who say, "There's enough to put right in this world without thinking about the next"? According to the Sermon on the Mount, it is by bringing the standards and ideals of "the blessed life" into our lives here and now that the life of society here and now will be lifted as yeast leavens the lump. It gives meaning also to the great prayer, *"Thy will be done on earth as it is in heaven."* "God is love," says a later New Testament writer: therefore His will is that we should make this world the school of Love in which rules and regulations are transcended. Dr. Charles Raven has summed it all up in one or two sentences.

"Our sole business is to love, and that cannot be done to order or by rule: we can only love as we share the Father's love. Love is not sentimentality: for sentimentality is the use of another for one's own emotional pleasure. . . . It is not passive acquiescence but a passion for comradeship in the adventure of living together, an intimate sympathy which involves a spontaneous and unreserved self-giving in interest and intuitive understanding." (*Jesus and the Gospel of Love*, p. 273.)

So the Sermon on the Mount ends on a practical note. One can almost see the great Teacher pause as he looks at the eager upturned faces of his disciples (for Matthew is careful to state that this teaching was given in the first instance to disciples only and not to the multitude), and he seems to be saying:

'Well, there is my teaching; there is a sketch of the kind of men and women the world of the future will need.

'Souls tempered with fire,
Fervent, heroic and good.'

It now remains for some of you to begin by acting upon what I have said.'

"*Everyone therefore that heareth these words of mine, and doeth them, will be like a wise man who built his house upon a rock: and the rain descended, and the floods came, and the winds blew and beat upon that house, and it fell not: for it was founded upon a rock.*"

Notice that he does not say a "good" man, but a "wise" man. His teaching is something more than morality. The Christian life is more than morality: it is practical spirituality; it is the life lived in the light, not of human experience which has been gathered up in laws, but in the light from lighter worlds than this, the light of the Divine wisdom itself.

And to turn away from that is not wickedness but simple folly: to build one's life on any other foundation but the Eternal is to build upon the shifting sands of time.

> "New occasions teach new duties,
> Time makes ancient good uncouth.
> They must upward still and onward,
> Who would keep abreast of Truth."

CHAPTER TWELVE

Every Man's Gospel

I SHOULD always recommend anyone who perhaps has not opened the New Testament lately to read the Third Gospel first. There are three obvious reasons for this. In the first place it is the most complete of all the Gospels and seems to have been written chiefly for Gentiles who would have little interest in the Jewish background of early Christianity: it has therefore the widest appeal. Secondly, it contains the great parables (notably those of the Prodigal Son and the Good Samaritan) which tell us more about the thoughts of Christ concerning God, man, and human life and destiny than any other single utterance: and these are nowhere else recorded. Thirdly, we can gather more information about the author, St. Luke, than about any other Biblical writer with the exception of St. Paul, whose letters are the earliest Christian writings that have come down to us. Although, of course, St. Luke was not one of the original disciples of Jesus (who were all Jews) and never saw the Master in the flesh, he must have come in touch with the Christian Movement (first known, as he alone tells us, as "The Way") at that most interesting and critical moment when the Gospel was first being preached to the Gentiles. He claims, in the short preface to his book, that he had received the bulk of his information from "*eyewitnesses and ministers of the word*" and that he "*traced the course of all things accurately from the first.*" That preface and a similar one introducing "The Acts of the Apostles," which also comes from his pen, gives a personal touch to his book which greatly adds to its interest for the modern reader.

From this and a good deal of other evidence, particularly certain sections of "The Acts" (Ch. 16: 10–18 and 20: 5–21: 18) which are introduced by the pronoun "WE" and are clearly part of his travel diary, one is left in no doubt that Luke was the Greek physician who travelled with St. Paul on his second great missionary journey and eventually accompanied him on his last journey

to Rome, where Paul says, *"only Luke is with me"* (II Tim. 4: 11).
From casual references to him in St. Paul's letters, it is also clear
that Luke was a well-known figure in the Early Church; so well
known, indeed, that in writing to the Corinthians Paul refers to
him anonymously as *"that brother whose services to the Gospel are
praised by all the Churches"* (II Cor. 8: 19). In the same letter, the
Apostle adds that Luke's appointment *"in connection with the
administration of the Charity* (for the home church at Jesusalem) *has
my full consent."*

In order to understand how Luke came to write his Gospel for
the Gentile world, we shall have to go back a little and try to see
how it was that he first heard of Christ. It all goes back to the first
important episode after the Crucifixion, which was the martyrdom of Stephen and the persecution which arose because of it.
Stephen was a young Greek convert appointed by the apostles as
a deacon, with six others, to administer relief to Christian widows.
We hear nothing more of the others but a great deal more about
this man Stephen, who became a preacher as well as an admini-
strator. The circumstances of his trial, the defence he made before
the Jewish Sanhedrin, and his subsequent martyrdom, are
extremely important because they show how the Gospel was first
made accessible to non-Jews.

The version of Christianity which Stephen preached was
something very different from that of the original apostles, Peter,
James and John. The charges brought against him are a clear indi-
cation of that. Although it is recorded that Stephen was condemned upon the evidence of "false witnesses," the charges which
he had to answer cannot have been wholly groundless however
much his actual message may have been distorted. He was accused
of having spoken words *"against this holy place"* (The Temple),
"against Moses" (The Law), and *"against God"* (i.e. orthodox
Jewish theology), and, most serious of all, he had said that *"this
Jesus of Nazareth shall change the customs delivered unto us"* (Acts 6).
Furthermore, the whole gist of his long speech before the Sanhedrin (Acts 7) bears this out. What Stephen had had to say about
the story of the Divine Revelation was nothing short of heresy to
Jewish ears. He had pointed out that God had made himself

known to their ancestors *before* they lived on the soil of the Holy Land. Abraham, the father of the faithful, had received his call when he was in Mesopotamia; Joseph and Moses had borne their witness to God in Egypt. (Mesopotamia and Egypt were Gentile lands, regarded by all good Jews as "unclean" and unsanctified lands.) And in his peroration Stephen had declared (as Isaiah and others had done before him) that "*the Most High dwelleth not in temples made with hands*" (Acts 7: 48).

All this was going a very long way beyond anything that Peter and the other apostles had ever said. Indeed, they had said nothing on these matters unacceptable to the Jewish authorities and had continued to associate themselves with Temple worship (Acts 3: 1–9). Their loyalty to the Church of their fathers was still unquestioned except for some rather strange and slightly unorthodox views which they had expressed about the crucified Nazarene whom they were proclaiming as the long expected Messiah and their queer notion regarding his Resurrection from the dead. Stephen was condemned and executed, therefore, by that Jewish political nationalism and narrow religious fanaticism which had always "stopped its ears" against the more spiritual and universalistic message of the prophets. Hence we are not surprised to read that the persecution which followed Stephen's death did not touch Peter and the original apostles. The Christians (of Stephen's school of thought) "*were scattered abroad, except the apostles*" (Acts 8: 1). Some of these reached Antioch. It must have been in Antioch or in one of those north Syrian cities that Luke the Greek doctor first heard of Christ. The version of the Gospel which he heard and received would therefore be that preached by the liberalising Christians of the School of Stephen. The whole of the Gospel which Luke subsequently wrote bears out that view. It fits in perfectly also with the whole story behind St. Paul's letter to the Galatians where he speaks of the trouble he had in opening the doors of the Christian Church to Gentiles. So sharp was his difference with the original apostles that on one occasion Paul says that he "withstood Peter to the face" (Gal. 2: 11).

It is impossible to fix the date of this or any other of the Gospels with absolute certainty, but we should be safe in assuming that St.

Luke wrote his book about ten years after the destruction of Jerusalem in A.D. 70. By that time the extensive missionary journeys of St. Paul had brought the Christian gospel out into the provinces of Asia Minor; that is, to the Gentile or pagan world. When we use the adjective "pagan" today we at once think of Atheists and out-and-out materialists who would deny any belief in a world of spiritual realities at all. The "pagan" world of St. Luke's day must not be thought of as resembling that. His readers, like St. Paul's audience at Athens, would consider themselves extremely religious people. In fact they were so keen to make contact with the spiritual world (which they believed in as intensely as modern people disbelieve in it) that many of them would be members of two or three or more of the popular religions (known to us as "mystery religions") which were all the rage in the cities of the Roman Empire of those days. Many of these, in particular Mithraism* and the cult of Attis and Osiris, were based on legends of a "saviour" God, by communion with whom, through elaborate rites and ceremonies, the worshippers hoped to insure immortality for themselves. So when St. Luke introduced them to the Gospel of Christ, it was perfectly natural that he should speak of Jesus as "saviour." He is the first of the Gospel writers to give Christ that title.

> "*Unto you is born this day in the City of David, a Saviour, which is Christ the Lord.*"

But whereas Mithra and Isis and the rest of the so-called "saviour gods" were admittedly legendary figures who gave their names to a cult, Jesus is immediately given an historical background. He was born in the reign of Caesar Augustus and his descent (through Joseph) is traced back to King David (3 : 31). Historically perhaps the genealogical tree may be of little value but its existence shows how great an importance this writer attached to proclaiming Jesus as a member of an actual human family—indeed of the whole human family, for he is not only the "son of David" but also "the son of Adam" (3 : 38).

But to St. Luke human history is not everything. Behind the

---

* Although Mithraism seems to have become popular at a later date than the others.

curtain of this visible world with its Emperors and its Kings and their courts and government departments, then as now ordering the affairs of men, is the invisible but equally real order of God and his angels. The language he uses in his account of the birth of Jesus to convey the activities of the spiritual world is not our language but it would not be strange to his readers of the first century. So he has no hesitation in telling them through the song of the angels that the unseen world is as much a reality as the fields of Bethelem to which the shepherds returned after having paid their homage to the heaven-born Prince of Peace.

The marriage of heaven and earth in the coming of Christ is expressed again in the beautiful songs which must be the writer's original compositions in Chapters 1 and 2. The songs of Mary (The Magnificat), Zacharias, the father of John the Baptist (The Benedictus), and the aged Simeon (The Nunc Dimittis) contain the same truth.

> *"My spirit hath rejoiced in God my Saviour"*
>
> *"The dayspring from on High hath visited us"*
>
> *"To be a light to lighten the Gentiles, and the glory of thy people Israel."*

The very word "Gentiles" (non-Jews) emphasises again the great universalistic feature of this Gospel.

We are now certain that all the Gospel writers made use of what is called "oral tradition" as well as written sources, and the latest school of thought lays very great emphasis upon its importance. So we can easily imagine this Greek doctor, during his visit to Palestine in company with St. Paul, visiting its towns and villages and gathering from all sorts of people their personal recollections of the deeds and words of Jesus. Of course it is impossible at this time of day to tell to what extent these narratives of Luke have preserved the actual words of Jesus or to what extent they are Luke's own "write-up." He certainly employed the technique of Thucydides, Plutarch and other ancient historians in composing speeches for his hero on various occasions and putting them into his mouth as though they were what he actually said at the time. This is very apparent in Luke's other work, the "Acts of the Apostles" (which we shall not have space to discuss in this book) and it must of course always be borne in mind. But we feel, as we read the account of the Sermon in the Nazareth synagogue (Luke 4), which led to the first attempt on Jesus' life at the hands of his fellow townsmen, that Luke wished to make clear to his readers that the hostility and bitterness of Jews towards Gentiles went right back to the very beginning. We certainly cannot imagine the very Jewish-minded editor of Matthew including such a story in his book.

Let us picture the scene which is so vividly portrayed in the middle of the fourth chapter. One Sabbath morning Jesus attends his local synagogue, probably the one he has attended since childhood. He is invited to read the lesson, and chooses a passage from Isaiah 61 which describes his own mission:

> *"The Spirit of the Lord God is upon me, because the Lord hath anointed me to preach good tidings unto the poor; he hath sent me to bind up the broken-hearted, to proclaim liberty to the captives, and the opening of the prison to them that are bound; to proclaim the acceptable year of the Lord. . . ."*

At that point, which is the middle of a sentence, Jesus folds up the roll and hands it back to the attendant. If he had read on, he would have read, *"to comfort all that mourn . . . to give them a garland for ashes, the oil of joy for mourning, the garment of praise for the spirit of heaviness."* But, although these beautiful phrases would have suited his purpose, he stopped short of them. Why? Obviously because the words, *"And the day of vengeance* (on the heathen) *of our God,"* came immediately after *"the acceptable year of the Lord."* One can picture certain devout members of the congregation pricking up their ears at that abrupt stopping point. "This man," they would be saying to themselves, "is no true patriot; he doesn't want God to pour out his indignation on the heathen Gentiles." When Jesus proceeds to expound that Scripture, their suspicions are confirmed by two references to Jewish history in which two of their great prophets, Elijah and Elisha, had been directly commissioned by God to show compassionate care for the heathen. Elijah was "sent" to look after a widow in *Zidon* during a famine; and Elisha cured Naaman, the commander in chief of the *Syrian* forces, of his leprosy. Jesus does not comment upon these incidents; he simply quotes them, but it is enough. Elders, scribes and congregation get up and hustle him out of the building and up the hill, where they try to throw him over the edge of a cliff.

I have no doubt that Luke is only giving a brief summary of the sermon which caused so much offence, but it is an excellent illustration of his skill as a writer, both in painting a picture and in selecting from popular talk in Nazareth thirty or forty years after the death of Jesus a characteristic episode showing his emancipated attitude towards the heathen. The unfriendly critic might feel inclined to interrupt with a protest here, and accuse Luke of writing biased history. On that point I shall quote Professor Trevelyan: "The problem of bias in history is fundamental and all-pervading. No one can write or teach history for ten minutes without coming in contact with the question, whether he is aware of it or not. Because history is not an exact science *but an interpretation of human affairs,** opinion and varieties of opinion intrude as inevitable factors. We cannot get rid of the element of opinion (or bias): we can, however, endeavour to make it the right kind of opinion—broad, all-embracing, philosophic—not a narrow kind that excludes half or more than half of reality." (*An Autobiography and Other Essays*, p. 68.) That, in the judgment of a modern historian, would justify St. Luke in his quite deliberate selection of stories which illustrate the universalist attitude of Jesus. It is as natural to him as it would be unnatural to a Jewish-minded editor like Matthew, to record that out of ten lepers there was only one who returned to express gratitude for his healing, "and he was a *Samaritan*." Again, other writers do not record the stern rebuke which Jesus administered to James and John, the sons of Zebedee, when they expressed the wish to "*call down fire from heaven*" on a "*Samaritan village*" which showed inhospitality to their Master. On the other hand, Luke does not conceal Christ's scorn of the

* Italics mine.

dictatorial and grandiose regime of the "Kings of the Gentiles" and of their condescending and superior attitude towards their subjects. It is he alone who records how Jesus told his disciples at the Last Supper, when they were quarrelling about precedence, that that sort of thing was quite contrary to the Spirit which should prevail amongst his followers. *"The Kings of the Gentiles exercise lordship over them; and they that have authority over them are called Benefactors. But ye shall not be so . . . I am among you as he that serveth."* (Luke 22: 25–27). This is a contrast for which the history of the Christian Church supplies a sad and pointed illustration. In his book *The Impatience of a Parson* (published 1927), H. R. L. Sheppard, the famous Vicar of St. Martin-in-the-Fields, suggested a number of resolutions which he hoped might be sunmitted to the Lambeth Conference of 1930. Amongst them was this:

"That the Anglican Communion is determined no longer to compete with the Kingdoms of this World for prestige. . . . It believes that titles such as "Your Grace" and "My Lord" must be renounced by the leaders of Anglicanism." His counsel was disregarded, but it was a striking example of the influence of St. Luke's Gospel in the twentieth century.

"He hath put down the mighty from their seat, and hath exalted the humble and meek."

No other Gospel has recorded incidents like the following, which represents Jesus so fully as the pioneer of a way of life in which human pride in any form has no place. It was pride which made it impossible for Simon the Pharisee to show the slightest appreciation of *"the woman that was a sinner"* (7). It was pride that make the elder brother exclude himself from the celebrations which attended the prodigal's return (15). It was pride, again, which turned the Pharisee's prayer into a boastful soliloquy upon his own good churchmanship—*"God, I thank thee that I am not as other men are."* In this Gospel Jesus is "The Saviour" of men and women because he is the servant of all the latent godlike qualities which are to be found, like a "treasure hidden in a field," in the heart of every man. He finds more of that treasure in people who are supposed to be beyond the pale, like Zaccheus (19) and the "publicans and sinners," than in those *"which trusted in themselves that they were righteous, and despised others"* (18: 9). It is significant that this writer, who alone records those words in the story of the Pharisee and the Publican, places next to it the incident of children being brought to Christ and his insistence upon the necessity of the unassuming attitude of childlikeness as the great qualification for entering the Kingdom. Any suggestion of staking a claim upon the favour of God because of one's merits or "good works" is promptly ruled out.

> *"Even so ye, when ye shall have done all the things which are commanded you, say, We are unprofitable servants: we have done that which it was our duty to do"* (Luke 17: 10).

Closely akin to this teaching is the teaching about the nature of the divine forgiveness proclaimed by Jesus, to which St. Luke draws very special attention. The other evangelists do not seem to have seized the point which Luke brings out so vividly, that the forgiveness of God does not wait upon human penitence but anticipates and stimulates it. The woman that was a sinner is told that *"her sins, which are many, are FORGIVEN; FOR SHE LOVED MUCH"* (or, "for her love is great"). She receives the divine forgiveness not because of her penitence but because of that very capacity for love which has previously been misdirected. Her "sins, which are many," are not in Jesus' estimation due to some innate wickedness but rather to the misuse of her greatest quality which will now be able to live and grow in her redeemed personality.

We see the same thing in Luke's record of the treatment of the thief on the cross. Matthew and Mark both tell us that there were "two others" crucified with Jesus, but it is Luke alone who has preserved the words of the criminal who said, *"Jesus, remember me when thou comest into thy Kingdom,"* and Jesus' reply, *"Verily I say unto thee, today shalt thou be with me in Paradise."*

All that the man had said was that he realised that he'd got what he deserved. That is hardly penitence, but it is the first step in the right direction and that is enough to kindle the healing flame of the divine compassion. Jesus, according to this writer, never bids the "fallen" man or woman bite the dust or humiliate themselves; he "bids the fallen sinner stand." He does not promise forgiveness when amends shall have been made, for he knows, as he said to Simon the Pharisee, that we are all "unable to pay"; he says that the forgiveness of God has already come running out to meet and heal us. That teaching, which in the Christian centuries has been "more honoured in the breach than in the observance," comes to full flower in the character of the Father in the story of the Prodigal Son. This story, recorded in St. Luke's fifteenth chapter and in no other Gospel, stands by itself in the literature of the world. Think for a moment of all the fantastic rites and ceremonies of purification which the initiates of the "mystery" religions of that time had to submit to; think of all the propitiatory sacrifices prescribed by the Jewish Church of that day; think of all the penances still imposed in the unreformed parts of the Christian Church and of all the mortifications of the flesh which men and women have inflicted upon themselves; then re-read the story of the Prodigal Son. The striking thing here is that the prodigal son, like the "penitent" thief, and the woman "that was a sinner," had only taken the first step in the right direction; yet

"when he was yet a great way off his father saw him, and had compassion, and ran, and fell on his neck and kissed him much."

(The Greek aorist tense of that verb might warrant us in translating it, "could not stop kissing him.") But that is not all. There is a still more wonderful touch which has often passed unnoticed. The boy begins the little speech which he has been composing on the way home, *"Father, I have sinned against heaven, and in thy sight I am no more worthy to be called thy son."* He is about to continue with, *"Make me as one of thine hired servants,"* but he is cut short and not allowed to humiliate himself before his father, who immediately loads him with gifts symbolic of his membership of the family from which he had thought himself excluded: the robe—no, the "best" robe—the shoes, and above all, the ring.

It is not too much to say that the figure of the father in this story gives us Jesus' most fundamental thought and experience of God. The rest of the story, which concerns the attitude of the elder son, underlines still more deeply that "the love of God is broader than the measures of man's mind." The elder son is offended at the suggestion that he should come in and take part in the celebrations on the occasion of his younger brother's re-instatement in the family circle—"*he was angry and would not go in.*" But the father shows no sign of offence or annoyance at his son's unbrotherly attitude. He "comes out" not to rebuke him but to "entreat"* him, and he tells him, in the tenderest words, that his attitude towards him is unaffected and unchanged: "*Son, thou art ever with me, and all that I have is thine.*"

But we owe to St. Luke not only this story which discloses Jesus' deepest thoughts of God, but also the story of the Good Samaritan, which gives us some of his most significant thoughts about man and his destiny. There is a very big point here in the setting of this famous story, which is often missed. The Good Samaritan who went out of his way to render "first-aid" and "after-care" to the wounded traveller has rightly become the patron saint of social service and all that goes by the name of prac-tical Christianity. He has given the charter to all the humanitarian reforms of the past nineteen hundred years. Without him we should have little with which to interpret the second great com-mandment, "*Thou shalt love thy neighbour as thyself.*" It was indeed Christ's answer to the question of the young theological student, "Who is my neighbour?" But the setting which St. Luke gives to the story is much wider than the road from Jerusalem to Jericho. The Priest and the Levite who ignored the wounded man and "by-passed" the spot where he lay, and the Good Samaritan who "came where he was" and attended to him, are not simply travellers on the roads of this world but travellers in eternity as well. For the student's original question was, "*What shall I do to inherit eternal life?*" The question of immortality was treated in the schools of the Rabbis no doubt as it is still so often treated today, as a highly theoretical and not very practical question hardly relevant to our day-to-day living. But the question was put

---

* The Greek word PARAKALEO is the same as that translated "Comforter" in the Fourth Gospel.

not in a theoretical but a practical form, *"What shall I do?"* and the answer which Jesus drew from him was equally practical— *"Thou shalt love the Lord thy God with all thy heart, with all thy soul, with all thy strength, and with all thy mind; and thy neighbour as thyself."* To love God with one's whole being, including the mind or intelligence ("with all thy mind"), and to love one's neighbour with all the intensity with which most men love themselves is, according to this teaching, what we must do to create a quality of life which will have what a scientist would call "survival value." In a word, it is the relationships which we form with other people which alone make life worth living in this world and the next.

This tallies with the other great parable which St. Luke alone has recorded, of Dives and Lazarus. The point of that story is also often missed. The rich man is pictured as "going through hell" in the next life, not because of his wealth in this, but because of his failure as a human being. That is the thing he is most aware of five minutes after death—*"the great gulf fixed"* between himself and the beggar Lazarus with whom he had never formed any link in the earth-life. It is not until he is officially dead and buried that he wakes up to the great realities of life here and hereafter, and expresses concern about his five brothers who are still missing their opportunities on earth as he had. So he asks that some arrangement should be made from that other world for their enlightenment—*"If one went unto them from the dead, they will repent."* He is told in reply that all the necessary means for their salvation have already been provided. *"They have Moses and the prophets, let them hear them."* The two great commandments which were the summary of "the Law and the Prophets" are "all on earth we need to know."

Finally, it is to St. Luke alone that we are indebted for the story of two other travellers on another road, who, according to him, were the first to have an experience of the Risen Christ. The story of the Emmaus road is unique. The oftener one reads it, the more does it seem to be something more than a story of the experience of the two disciples who are mentioned in it. The problem which was occupying their minds and their conversation was the major problem which these first Christians had to solve—"How can the sufferings and crucifixion of Jesus be reconciled with his Messiah-ship?" As Jews they had been led to believe that the Messiah of their national expectations would be a triumphant conqueror who would lead the armies of Israel to victory over all their enemies and establish the sovereignty of God over all nations. We over-hear this hope from one of the travellers on the road to Emmaus: "*We hoped that it should have been he* (Jesus) *who should have redeemed Israel.*" In reply to this, the Risen Jesus answers, "*Behoved it not the Messiah to suffer and so to enter into his glory?*" After that we are told that he "*opened to them in all the Scriptures the things concerning himself.*" But even after this great exposition of the suffering Messiah (no doubt from Isa. 53), although "*their hearts burned within them,*" it took the familiar gesture of the "*breaking of the bread*" finally to convince them that it was indeed their beloved Master who had "*made himself known to them.*" I think that St. Luke is attempting through this great story of the Emmaus road to record in a highly dramatic form the way in which the truth of Jesus' resurrection gradually came home first to their minds (through a fresh reading of their Scriptures, especially Isa. 53) and then to their spiritual perception and experience "in the breaking of bread." If my suggestion can be accepted, St. Luke has given us here good news for every man—the presence of the living Christ through the New Testament Scriptures for the convincing of our minds, and the "breaking of the bread" in the Holy Communion for the strengthening and refreshing of our souls.

CHAPTER THIRTEEN

A Gospel of Experience

IT is difficult for us to imagine a Christian missionary setting out to carry the Gospel into the heathen world without a copy of the four Gospels in his kit. But that is how it was with St. Paul. The only Scriptures that he took with him were the Old Testament Scriptures in the Greek version (The Septuagint), and these would not be of very much use to him except when he was preaching Christ in Jewish synagogues.

We can be certain of this because of dates. St. Paul was executed during the persecution of the Christians under the Emperor Nero in A.D. 62 or 63, and the earliest possible date for St. Mark's Gospel (the earliest of the four) is A.D. 65. That goes a long way to explain why in his letters, which are the earliest Christian documents in our possession, Paul never quotes any of the sayings of Jesus with which the Gospels subsequently made people familiar. But that was not so great a disadvantage as we might imagine. The motley crowds which gathered around a travelling missionary in the market place of Ephesus or Colossae, or outside a heathen temple in the country districts of Galatia or on the wharves of Corinth, would not be in the least impressed by hearing a speaker quote from books they'd never heard of. The only thing likely to hold a crowd in the open air is something out of the speaker's own experience. That was the very thing that Paul had to offer them. His message was based on the main facts of Christ's life, death and resurrection; but the heart of what he had to say concerned the new kind of life which was within reach of those who came to believe in Christ as the "Lord from heaven"—Christ who makes a new man of anyone who will receive his life-giving spirit. "*If any man is in Christ he is a new creature*." He was equally emphatic in asserting that without this vital contact with the living spirit of Christ no one can claim the name of Christian. "*If any man have not the Spirit of Christ, he is none of his*" (Rom. 8: 9).

So we can say that Paul's gospel was a gospel of experience.

The creeds and dogmas which have been constructed from these letters of his have again and again obscured from the ordinary reader the simplicity and vital spiritual teaching which they contain. The Authorised Version of 1611, with its superb diction, often hides from us the telling phrases which he used in the colloquial Greek of the market-place to convey to all men the newly discovered power by which he lived. Much of this original freshness and force has now been given back to us through the work of modern translators. Of these, I think Dr. James Moffatt's translation is still the best. So before we enquire into St. Paul's personal experience which was the mainspring of his whole Gospel, let me emphasise by a few illustrations the importance of reading him in modern speech. You see, the Greek in which Paul wrote was, as I have said, not the dignified classical language of Plato and Aristotle, but corresponded to the kind of English we use in a religious broadcast in the Home Service or on the Light Programme. This is so very different from the stately style of the Authorised Version of the Bible that at first people hardly recognise it as coming from the Bible at all. I remember the first time I read the Hymn of Love in I Corinthians 13 to a hospital staff, using Dr. Moffatt's translation, there was a storm of protest. "We want the Bible: not that stuff!" they said. It is true, of course, that one misses the beauty of the seventeenth century prose, but how much more important it is to get at the real meaning. It is forgotten, too, that Moffatt or any other modern translator has access to early manuscripts which had not been discovered in 1611, and also to contemporary papyri rescued from the dust heaps of Egypt in the present century, which throw a whole flood of light upon the Greek words which Paul and everybody else used at that time. That means that in many places the Authorised Version, besides wrapping up the plain words of Paul in fine phrases, actually mistranslates him. In the letter to the Philippians, for example, he tells them of his prayer for them. The Authorised Version renders Chapter 1: 10, "*That ye may approve things that are excellent,*" which would simply mean "approving of what is good," a rather dull platitudinous expression. But Moffatt gives us what the Greek word for "approve" really meant in those days.

It was used in connection with the testing of metals. He also gives the real meaning of the Greek word rendered "excellent," which really meant "that which excels in importance." Putting all that together, Moffatt renders it, *"enabling you to have a sense of what is vital,"* which is a very different and much more important thing. Another important alteration is to be found in I Corinthians 13 : 7, where we have: *"Charity beareth all things, believeth all things, hopeth all things, endureth all things."* Perfect rhythm, but surely perilous counsel too often followed by pious and unthinking persons whose credulity is such that they will believe anything. Moffatt has restored the apostle's good Christian counsel by translating "believing all things" as, *"always eager to believe the best."* But sometimes the Authorised Version is just unintelligible. This is especially the case in II Corinthians—a letter brimming over with passion, pain, and pleading, in which Paul is opening his inmost heart and unbaring his very soul. Here is a most intimate and telling passage, but I defy anyone to feel this from the Authorised Version, which reads:

> "O ye Corinthians, our mouth is open unto you, our heart is enlarged.
>
> Ye are not straitened in us, but ye are straitened in your own bowels.
>
> Now for a recompense in the same (I speak as unto my children), be ye also enlarged."

What on earth can he mean by that? Moffatt makes it as clear as daylight (2 Cor. 6: 11–13):

> *"O Corinthians, I am keeping nothing back from you; my heart is wide open for you. 'Restraint'?—that lies with you, not me. A fair exchange, now, as the children say! Open your hearts wide to me."*

Lastly, on this point of modern translations, there is given back to us something of the urgency which belongs to a letter which is being written at top speed while the messenger is waiting. We know that the two Corinthian letters are only a fragment of the correspondence which passed between the Apostle and this young Christian community which caused him so much anxiety and called forth such frankness from him. In this case I will not transcribe the Authorised Version but only Dr. Moffatt's vivid rendering (2 Cor. 11: 16–21):

> "*I repeat, no one is to think me a fool; but even so, pray bear with me, fool as I am, that I may have my little boast as well as others! (What I am now going to say is not inspired by the Lord: I am in the rôle of a 'fool,' now, on this business of boasting. Since many boast on the score of the flesh, I will do the same.) You put up with fools so readily, you who know so much! You put up with a man who assumes control of your souls, with a man who spends your money, with a man who dupes you, with a man who gives himself airs, with a man who flies in your face. I am quite ashamed to say I was not equal to that sort of thing!*"

I don't think anyone can help feeling the throb of the man's personality in that, and no one would want to go back for the meaning to the Authorised Version in which it is completely obscured.

The Galatian letter, too, is clearly written in the heat of the controversy with those who have been interfering with his young converts and trying to impose upon them the rules and regulations of the Jewish Law. One can almost see Paul seizing the pen (or stylus) from the weary hand of his secretary Tychicus so that there shall be no lack of vigour in his last paragraph. "*See what big letters I make, when I write you in my own hand!*" (Gal. 6: 11)—and he must have nearly pressed the pen through the paper as he wrote his final sentence, "*Let no one interfere with me after this, for I bear branded on my body the owner's stamp of the Lord Jesus.*" (Gal. 6: 17).

But the uninstructed reader of this letter to the young Churches of Galatia might well ask, "Why all this vehemence? Can the writer of this letter be a true interpreter of the Prince of Peace? Is he not a highly-strung and even bitter controversialist?" What lies behind such language as this in the fourth chapter, verses 19 and 20: "*O my dear children, you with whom I am in travail over again till Christ be formed within you, would that I could be with you*

A Gospel of Experience

at this moment, and alter my tone, for I am at my wits' end about you!"

To understand and appreciate this is to go a long way to understanding and appreciating St. Paul and a good deal of vital Christianity as well. The key to it all is to be found in that basic spiritual experience which we call his "Conversion," and which at the beginning of this letter he refers to as his "revelation." *"Brothers,"* he writes, *"I tell you the Gospel that I preach is not a human affair; no man put it into my hands, no man taught me what it meant; I had it by a revelation of Jesus Christ"* (Gal. 1: 11–12). His own word "revelation" is probably a better word than "conversion" to describe his experience. We generally associate conversion with turning over a new leaf, or forsaking an immoral life for a moral one and becoming a reformed character. But that would totally misrepresent the case of St. Paul. The change that came in his life was not from a bad life to a good one but from a good life to a better. Saul of Tarsus, as he himself explains, had been brought up as a Pharisee and a very strict Pharisee at that. The Pharisees were by far the most spiritually-minded sect of the Jews. Many of them, it is true, had become so wrapped up in the observance of non-essentials that they had lost touch with the things that matter most—mercy and truth. Many of them answered to the description which Jesus gave of them as those who *"trusted in themselves that they were righteous and despised others."* In a word, there were a good many spiritual snobs among them. But that can hardly have been true of them all. It is a well-known fact that the corruption of the best is always the worst. So when Saul the Pharisee became Paul the Christian he exchanged a highly moral and spiritual faith for something better. How was it better and what was it that brought about the change in him? Once more I think the word "Revelation" is better than "Conversion," because conversion usually suggests something sudden, and Paul's experience was not a sudden happening. It was, like the whole of God's Revelation, a gradual and progressive experience. In one of his last letters (Philippians) he writes, *"Not that I have already attained this or am already perfect, but I press forward to appropriate it, . . . Brothers, I for one do not consider myself to have appropriated this; my one thought is, by forgetting what lies behind me and straining to what*

*lies before me, to press on to the goal for the prize of God's high call in
Christ Jesus"* (Phil. 3 : 12–13).

Where then did it begin? Luke, his private physician and travelling companion, who later wrote the Acts of the Apostles, leaves
us in no doubt. In his account of Paul's great speech to the crowd
in Jerusalem preceding his final arrest, the historian puts these
words into his mouth. *"While I was praying in the temple I fell into a
trance and saw Him* (Christ) *saying to me, 'Make haste, leave Jerusalem
quickly, for they will not accept your evidence about me.' But, 'Lord,' I
said, 'they surely know it was I who imprisoned and flogged those who
believed in you . . . and that I stood and approved when the blood of
your martyr Stephen was being shed, taking charge of the clothes of his
murderers!' "* (Acts 22: 17–20).

It was what Stephen had taught that had roused Paul's worst
passions. He would have had but little objection to the older
apostles, Peter and James and John, who at that time still maintained their connection with the Jewish Church and were only
suspect in the eyes of the Jewish authorities because they had the
strange idea that the crucified Nazarene was the long-promised
Messiah. But Stephen had gone very much further than that.
Stephen had said in effect that Christianity and Judaism were like
oil and water and that Jesus would destroy the Temple and all that
it stood for and *"change the customs delivered by Moses."* But although Stephen's speech was bound to arouse his persecuting zeal
as a Jew and a Pharisee, and although *"Saul quite approved of his
murder"* (Acts 7), there was something else that aroused very
different feelings. A man who could pray for his murderers as the
stones fell thick and fast about him, a man who as he was being
slowly battered to death could declare that he could see, right
through the veil into heaven, *"Jesus standing at God's right hand,"*
must have something in him. Could he, Saul, take *his* death like
that? Perhaps, if he could see what Stephen said he saw. Paul's
immediate reaction was to re-double his efforts to stamp out the
dangerous movement. But as the weeks went by, other questions
began to trouble him. Could Stephen and these Christians whom
he was rounding up for execution possibly be right after all? Was
it possible that they were in possession of a secret still hidden from

him? They certainly had a poise and a peace that he, Saul, had never known. That was the conflict and the struggle which was finally resolved on the road a few miles out of Damascus, where he was going with the High Priests' commission to extirpate the Christians. It was this which finally brought about the conversion of Saul the Pharisee into Paul the Apostle of Jesus Christ. It was this that made a Christian of him and, as Dean Inge truly said, it was "to the Christianity of Stephen and not to that of James, the Lord's brother, that he was converted."

That accounts for the whole theme of the Galatian letter which is now held to be the earliest of all his letters and may easily have been written as early as A.D. 45 or 46. It also accounts for the vehemence and urgency with which he writes. The background of the Epistle to the Galatians was this. The home Church of Peter and the original Jewish disciples had taken alarm at the missionary activities of Paul among the Gentiles. They felt that what he was preaching was a kind of watered-down gospel. So they had sent out what they regarded as a mission of help to Paul's infant Churches. In brief, they told his young converts that they must become good Jews before they could hope to be good Christians. They must submit to all the rites and ordinances of the Jewish Church (including circumcision). That is the situation which called forth the astonishment and indignation of the opening chapter. "*I am astonished that you are hastily shifting like this, deserting Him who called you by Christ's grace and going over to another gospel. It simply means that certain individuals are unsettling you; they want to distort the Gospel of Christ*" (Gal. 1: 8). That is a direct counter-attack on the mission of help from Jerusalem, which Paul rightly regarded as a wicked piece of interference. "*Whoever preaches a gospel to you that contradicts the gospel I preached to you, God's curse be on him!*" The antithesis between Judaism and Christianity is sharply stated at the beginning of Chapter 5. "*Here, listen to Paul! I tell you, if you get circumcised, Christ will be no use to you.*" As for himself, he says, Christianity means one thing and one thing only, whatever anybody else may say: "*The life I now live in the flesh, I live by faith in the Son of God who loved me and gave himself up for me*" (Gal. 2: 20). To tell anyone who has that knowledge and certainty to go back to a Judaistic form of Christianity, would be like telling a young freshman who has just entered the University that he has got to go back to his prep. school! Indeed, that is precisely the light in which Paul had come to regard "The Law" (Judaism). *"The law was our schoolmaster to bring us to Christ."*

That brings us to St. Paul's greatest contribution to the Christian faith which he elaborated in the Epistle to the Romans. Theology has made it all very complicated, but like other profound truths it is really very simple. Paul was concerned, from the moment when he first began to know Christ, with the central problem of human life, because for him Christ had solved it. That problem is the management of one's inner life of thought and instinct. In this, Paul had found that Judaism, "The Law" as he calls it, had completely let him down. *"The good that I would I do not: but the evil which I would not, that I do."* (You should read the whole of Romans 7, which is from verse 7 onwards a piece of autobiography.) Worse than that, it had been a hindrance to his spiritual progress and not a help. He says, for instance, that it kept putting wrong ideas into his head. The tenth commandment, he says, was responsible for suggesting to his mind the idea of covetousness and gave him an impulse to sin, just as the notice "Trespassers will be prosecuted" has often incited a boy to go birds-nesting in a particular wood. He can never forget that Christ was crucified not by pagans who "knew not the law" but by the Jewish authorities who did. Therefore it followed that it was just those very sins which the Law had been unsuccessful in preventing which had led to the greatest crime in history. What were those sins? They all boiled down to one—Pride (Pride of nation, Pride of Church, Pride of self).

"None of the Powers of this world" had understood that, *"for if they had, they would never have crucified the Lord of Glory"* (I Cor. 2: 8).

That was the fundamental difference between Judaism and Christianity. The Law could not deal with the deadliest of the seven deadly sins—human pride—and Christ had and could. And Christ had dealt with it in an entirely new way. The Law had tried punishing the offender, but God in Christ had himself taken all the punishment upon himself. That is what Paul meant when he talked of Christ *"dying for our sins,"* or of himself as being *"crucified with Christ."* I do not believe that he ever meant to suggest that Christ offered a propitiatory sacrifice to save men from the wrath of God (this was an idea taken over from the heathen sacrifices which has poisoned Christian theology all through the centuries). He really meant that Christ's wonderful spirit of love and self-sacrifice in accepting all that had been done to him had inspired him to "pour contempt on all his pride."

Paul could easily have been the biggest egotist in history and as great a peril to the human race as Napoleon or Hitler, but Christ had saved him from himself. *"I was once,"* he writes, *"immaculate by the standard of legal righteousness, but for Christ's sake I have learned to count all my former gains a loss; indeed I count everything a loss, compared to the supreme value of knowing Christ Jesus my Lord"* (Phil. 3). Through those revealing words Paul shows that he had found the secret of consecrated personality, the *"I, yet not I."* He could therefore talk about his labours and his achievements for the Gospel as exceeding those of any of the other apostles—*"I laboured more abundantly than they all"*—simply because it came quite naturally to him to add immediately, *"Yet not I, but the grace of God which was with me"* (I Cor. 15). That is the very heart of the Gospel which he preached and which is still available to us through his letters. Every religious revival has been and always will be a return to that. I do not think that the old phrase, "Justification by faith" is of very much value to us; the experience which it covers must be described in our own terms. There is hardly a better summary of it than that of Archbishop William Temple who once compared Judaism with plodding up a long winding staircase with the feeling that one will never reach the top and Christianity with getting on to a moving staircase. St. Paul called it living and moving *"in a new sphere of life"* (Rom. 6 : 4). This is the Gospel with which we shall be able to answer the "humanist" who is always pouring scorn (not unjustifiably) upon the dogmas and the legends which he identifies with Christianity. We shall never convince anybody at this time of day by appealing to facts, however impressive or well authenticated, but only to that stream of Christian experience which has flowed down through the centuries as the Spirit of Christ, which Paul identifies with the Spirit of the living God.

But what, we must ask finally, does Paul mean by the Spirit of Christ? This we can only learn by reading these letters over and over again, for it breathes from almost every line that he wrote. All that I can do in this short chapter is to direct your attention to a few passages which no one ought to miss. The first of these is the whole of the letter to Philemon, which is the shortest complete letter we have. It is the kind of letter which would be marked "Private and Confidential." It is all about a slave boy called Onesimus, and is addressed by Paul to a friend named Philemon with whom he had stayed in Colossae. I have chosen this because it illustrates so clearly how the Spirit of Christ was brought to bear by St. Paul upon a very common everyday situation. It also gives us a very vivid glimpse of life in these early Churches. When I say "Churches," you must not picture buildings, for of these there were none. Christianity was for its first 300 years a "religio illicita" or forbidden religion in the Roman Empire; it was what we should call an "underground movement," and meetings of believers had to be held in private houses. Such a house was the home of Philemon at Colossae. In writing to him Paul greets not only the family of Philemon but also *"the Church that meets in your house."* So "the Church" here means the Christian fellowship. Every man of means in a city like Colossae would have a staff of perhaps forty or fifty slaves, some of whom would be more educated men who would be tutors to the children, while others would be domestics or labourers on the estate or employed in the dye works or at the weaving looms which were often attached to great houses. (Discoveries of contemporary Roman villas like the one at Chedworth in Gloucestershire have shown this.) Now, among Philemon's household slaves was a boy with the Greek name of Onesimus (which means "worthy" or "useful"). It is quite likely that this slave-boy had had a glimpse of St. Paul and had possibly overheard some conversation about Christ during the Apostle's visit to his master. An impression must somehow have been made on his mind which Onesimus never forgot. Some years afterwards when Paul was in prison at Rome, Onesimus got into some sort of trouble and ran away from his master, eventually arriving in the great city where no one would recognise him. Here, wandering in the streets of Rome, we must assume that he was befriended by some members of the Christian fellowship who brought him to Paul. No record remains of what must have passed between them. All that we have is this little note with which the Apostle sent him back to his old master Philemon. Quite apart from the letter itself, which even in translation gives us a breath of the atmosphere of faith in the power of the Spirit and deep human understanding in which these people lived, the fact of this difficult reconciliation speaks for itself. It is just one instance of the ministry of reconciliation which was going on every hour of the day. St. Paul through the power of the Spirit had made a new man of Onesimus. This is the main point in his letter. "*I appeal to you on behalf of my spiritual son born while I was in prison. It is Onesimus* (Worthy)." Paul then makes a pun on his name: "*Once you found him a worthless character, but nowadays he is worth something to you and me.*" The rest of it repays close study because it shows how those who really have the Spirit of Christ can not only restore broken relationships but build up and strengthen one another through mutual service at the deepest level. Paul has started to make a new man of a hitherto "worthless character." Philemon is to continue the good work. "*Perhaps this was why you and he were parted for a while that you might get him back for good, no longer a mere slave but something more than a slave—a beloved brother; especially dear to me but how much more to you as a man and as a Christian! You count me a partner? Then receive him as you would receive me.*" His next words open up another story which must be left to our imagination, for it is the story of Philemon himself and his conversion. Paul reminds him of it in the kindliest possible way. "*If he* (Onesimus) *has cheated you of any money or owes you any sum, put that down to my account. This is in my own handwriting: 'I Paul promise to refund it'.*" (How could a man in prison have any cash at his disposal? But the next sentence quickly removes any financial obligation!) "*Not to mention that you owe me, over and above, your very soul.*" And this mention of

Philemon's debt to him makes him add quickly that both of them owe an unpayable debt to Christ. "*Come, brother, let me have some return from you in the Lord! Refresh my heart in Christ. . . . The grace of the Lord Jesus Christ be with your spirit.*" Nothing can really come of it all without the grace or help which flows into their lives from the Spirit of Christ, but all can be done through Christ who strengthens them (see Phil. 4: 10–13).

From all this, then, we learn that Paul's gospel or good news is the practical experience of the enabling power of the spirit of Christ which is the Spirit of Reconciliation. This is the thing with which he says God "*has entrusted me*" (2 Cor. 5: 19). I have drawn your attention to this practical example of the effectiveness of "the Spirit of Christ" because people so often think it is just a pious phrase which religious people use, meaning little more than good nature or kind-heartedness.

> "So many Gods, so many creeds,
> So many paths that wind and wind,
> When just the art of being kind
> Is all this sad world needs."

It is true that the world needs more kindness, but to say that this is all the world needs is a terrible understatement. Day by day those of us who know that we are entrusted with this gospel of reconciliation and try to put it into operation find that people need infinitely more than mere kindness or good nature. If we didn't believe that, we should soon find ourselves going back to some form of Pharisaism or self-culture or self-effort or what in the modern world is called "humanism." That would be to forget the whole lesson which St. Paul first learnt in his own life and then handed on to others, that in the major tasks of life we have little or no power to help ourselves, and our sufficiency (or efficiency) is of God who has, as he says, made us "*able ministers of the New Covenant,*" which is Christianity, as distinct from Judaism or any other religion.

CHAPTER FOURTEEN

The Gospel of the Greater Works of Christ

ANYONE who sits down for half an hour with the Gospel according to St. John can tell that he is reading quite a different kind of
book from the other three gospels—indeed, quite a different kind
of book from any other in the world. We should look at it in the
same frame of mind in which we view great works of art, for
John's spiritual truths strike home not through historical facts but
through the dramatic tableaux he brings to life before us to
reveal the very essence of Christ's personality and the wideness of
his mission.

That this is the only right approach is confirmed at once by the
earliest description of its origin, preserved by the historian
Eusebius who wrote, "John, last of all, perceiving that what had
reference to the body in the Gospel of our Saviour was sufficiently
detailed, and being urged by his familiar friends, urged also by the
Spirit, wrote a *Spiritual Gospel*." John himself says, in the last
words of his twentieth chapter, that his main purpose in writing
his book was to put new life into us. *"These are written that ye may
believe that Jesus is the Christ, the Son of God; and that believing ye
may have Life through his name."*

We cannot be far wrong in assuming with Professor C. H.
Dodd of Cambridge and other scholars that this John was "John
the Elder," a greatly revered teacher in the Church of Ephesus at
the very end of the first century. John the son of Zebedee, the
Apostle of Christ, certainly comes into the story as the "beloved
disciple" (12: 25, etc.) but it is equally certain that the highly
philosophical prologue (1: 1–18) and the whole style and content
of the book could not possibly have come from a Galilean fisherman, however inspired.

Viewed against the background of Ephesus in the last years of
the first century, when the Christian Church was face to face not
only with rival religions (like Mithraism) but also with the whole
system of thought which we know as Gnosticism (claiming

special knowledge of spiritual mysteries), the Fourth Gospel will be best understood as the first and boldest restatement of the Gospel of Christ. The vividness of some of the narratives has led many people to think that the writer's interest was mainly historical, but a closer examination of the historical incidents which he includes will show that this was not so. Matthew, Mark and Luke had recorded the actual deeds and words of Jesus, and John certainly had their books in front of him as he wrote; but his treatment of historical events is more that of a dramatist than of an historian. We will take one illustration of that.

According to the other three Evangelists, the last public act of Jesus was the Cleansing of the Temple. This took place on Palm Sunday. It was the final protest of Jesus against the type of religion represented by the Temple. No sooner had he driven out the vendors of the sacrificial victims and declared that his Father's house was meant to be not merely a national but an international place of prayer *"for all nations,"* than the chief priests and the scribes went into committee to arrange for his death. The Temple and all that it stood for was felt to be in danger.

> *"And the scribes and chief priests heard it, and sought how they might destroy him: for they feared him"* (Mark 11 : 18).

But John takes this incident which everybody knew to be the direct cause of the arrest, trial and death of Jesus, and gives his version of it right at the very beginning, before the public ministry of Jesus. What can have been his purpose in doing this? Well, to begin with, by the time John wrote his Gospel, the very Temple which Jesus had cleansed had been actually destroyed (A.D. 70). Furthermore, the attempt on the part of Jewish Christians to adulterate the Gospel with Jewish traditions and observances had been frustrated by the emancipating work of St. Paul. Had he not in his letter to the Church in Ephesus* declared that the Christian community itself was to become "A holy temple in the Lord," of which Jesus himself was "the chief corner stone"? All of that lies

---

* Some scholars are of the opinion that "Ephesians" is not actually written by the Apostle, but its thought seems to me thoroughly Pauline.

behind John's picture of the Cleansing of the Temple. In his presentation of it (and in his presentation alone) Jesus in reply to his critics challenges them in the words, "Destroy this temple, and in three days I will raise it up." The Jews protest that the Temple took forty-six years to build and that it was therefore ridiculous to suggest that it could be rebuilt in three days. But John immediately adds that Jesus was speaking of "the temple of his body" and that this was fully understood only after his Resurrection (on the third day). Can there be any doubt whatever that the writer's purpose was to proclaim a spiritual truth through a semi-historical or dramatic picture? That truth was that the Risen Christ and the Christian community in which his spirit dwells is the true Temple through which, as Paul had taught we have access to the Father. He expressed the same truth later in his Gospel—*"No man cometh unto the Father, but by me"* (14). He put this picture in the forefront of his Gospel because of its paramount spiritual importance.

If we had nothing else but this spiritual treatment of the historical fact of the Cleansing of the Temple, it would be enough to show how closely John keeps to his terms of reference to write a Spiritual Gospel. But we have much more. There are, in all, seven historical or semi-historical highly dramatic pictures in this book. They are:

1. The Marriage Feast of Cana. (2: 1)
2. The Healing of the Nobleman's son. (4: 46)
3. The Healing of the Impotent Man at Bethesda. (5: 1)
4. The Feeding of the Five Thousand. (6: 5)
5. The Walking on the Water. (6: 15)
6. The Restoration of Sight to a Man. (9: 1)
7. The Raising of Lazarus. (11)

Now, the fact that John's purpose in recording these incidents was spiritual and not historical is made clear to us at once by the writer himself. He calls them all "SIGNS." They are not just stories of fact, but stories with a certain spiritual meaning or significance. They are not bald statements of what the historical Jesus did, but illustrations of what the living Christ is always doing. In them,

John is doing for Jesus the same sort of thing that Shakespeare did for King Henry V, or John Drinkwater did for Abraham Lincoln. Indeed, the last words of Drinkwater's play, "Now he belongs to the Ages," would give them an appropriate title.

It is most unfortunate that our Authorised Version translated the Greek word SĒMEION as "Miracle." SĒMEION is the Greek for a Sign. The Revised Version (1881) gives the right translation. That one word, "Sign," restores the sense in which John intended them to be taken.

This is specially important in the case of the first and the last of these "Signs," the Marriage Feast at Cana in Galilee and the Raising of Lazarus. If one takes these as miracles in the literal sense (in which they have usually been taken) they will become obstacles instead of aids to faith. But when they are taken symbolically, they provide an excellent commentary on the words of the Prologue, *We beheld his glory*." Thus understood they will give us the key to the understanding of St. John's Gospel.

At the end of the story about the Marriage Feast in Cana we read,

"*This beginning of his signs did Jesus in Cana of Galilee, and manifested forth his glory; and his disciples believed on him.*" (2 : 11)

So the story of the water which was made wine is a "sign" story, or, as we should say, a significant story through which the author is going to tell us something which is intended to show the "glory" of Jesus. The word "glory" in Greek really means "character." It is a favourite word of John's. Therefore, if we were to accept this story literally as a miracle by which Jesus turned 120 gallons of water into wine, we should have to say that this was a manifestation of his character and that because of it his disciples came to believe in him. But this would be contradictory to the whole impression given us by the other Gospels of the attitude of Jesus towards those who demanded miracles of just that kind. Also it would be totally inconsistent with Jesus' own rejection of that method of proving his divine mission (see the narrative of the Temptation, in St. Luke 4 : 10–12). The purpose of Jesus, according to John, was to reveal to men God's character (glory) and ways of working. So if we were to accept this story at its face value it would be simply a piece of magical display. We should then have to believe that God really does work in that kind of way. But nothing in this book (which, remember, according to the Author's purpose is a "Spiritual Gospel") should ever be taken at its face value or literally. *"The letter killeth, but the Spirit giveth life."* I once saw in a Church a stained-glass window which depicted Jesus standing over a servant who is pouring water from a jug into one of the six huge jars which are standing on the floor. Exactly half-way between the lip of the jug and the brim of the jar, the jet of water suddenly turns bright red! That is exactly the kind of interpretation which Bernard Shaw had in mind when he called Jesus "The Conjurer."

How then did John intend us to interpret the story? Undoubtedly as a "sign" or symbol of certain important truths about Jesus and his gospel. First and foremost he wished to show, as the other evangelists (especially St. Mark, the earliest of them) had shown, that Jesus was the most human of men and entered wholeheartedly into all human joys and festivities. He called himself (as contrasted with John the Baptist) "the Son of Man, who came eating and drinking." This had given rise to criticism from some of the strait-laced Pharisees who thought that it was unseemly for a Rabbi to behave in this way. Mark records that on one occasion (representative of many), when some of them had remonstrated with Jesus for disregarding an official Fast (like Lent), he replied by asking whether brides and bridegrooms and their friends usually don sackcloth and ashes on their wedding day. By that Jesus obviously meant to suggest that he and his disciples were living all the time in the spirit of wedding guests, who make the most and the best of everything.

Now John had a particular reason for wishing to give prominence to this particular aspect of the "glory" or character of Jesus. In Ephesus and elsewhere at the time when he was writing, there was a school of thought known as GNOSTICISM (Greek GNOSIS = knowledge) which regarded all material things as evil in themselves and taught that the less a Christian has to do with the physical side of life the better. They also taught that Jesus was not really human at all but a phantom. So the setting of a village wedding was more than apt. The idea of a great spiritual teacher going to a wedding feast would be quite as shocking to a Gnostic as going to a dance was to a Puritan later on. Next John would see that in the same passage from Mark (2: 18–22) Jesus had spoken symbolically of his teaching, as contrasted with Judaism, as *"NEW WINE."* Further, in Luke's version of the same saying (Luke 5: 39) Jesus had humorously added that he was afraid that his "new wine" would in all probability not be very readily welcomed. *"No one wants new wine immediately after drinking old; 'The old,' he says, 'is better'."*

Now two generations had passed since Jesus had said these things, and the conflict between the Gospel—the new teaching— and the old tradition of Judaism was practically over. But there must have been some who still kept hankering after the time-honoured traditions of the parent faith. John recognises it in his first sentence.

"And the Mother of Jesus was there."

I think John intended her to represent the Jewish Church and those to whom its traditions were still very dear. Paul, as we have seen, had had to deal very sharply with them in the heat of controversy (see his letter to the Galatians) but now that the unhappy conflict was nearly over John finds "the more excellent way." He makes the Jewish traditionalists confess (through "the Mother of Jesus," the "Mother" Church) that the old vintage has failed.

"The Mother of Jesus saith unto him, they have no wine." (The old teaching has dried up.)

Every word here tells. Jesus will not press people to accept him and his teaching too quickly. He replies most gently and tactfully, *"Is that your concern or mine?"* (Phillips' translation), and adds, *"Mine hour is not yet come."* (That means, "It's no use unless you think that the hour has struck for my teaching to supersede Judaism.") Upon this, the Mother of Jesus gives the instructions to the "servants" (obviously the disciples), *"Mind you do whatever he tells you.*" They then pour the water into the jars (which were connected with Jewish purification rites) and offer it to the Master of Ceremonies, who would of course be a Jew and not yet a Christian. He tastes it. In other words, he drinks of the Gospel, "the living water" (as John elsewhere calls it). One sip convinces him. "Why," he says, "this is astonishing! Our usual custom is to serve guests from the rich old vintage first because it is usually the more potent, and then, when that is exhausted and when men have well drunk, we give them the newer and less potent wine; but here today you have kept the good wine until last."

John finishes the story by telling his readers that the Gospel, although a much simpler religion than Judaism (as water is a simpler liquid than wine), is just as capable of making glad the heart of man.

But the other "Signs" will carry us much further. Jesus, the "Word" or expression in human form of the Eternal Mind of God (1:14) has been sent into the world for one supreme purpose. This is stated in the great words of the "Good Shepherd" (another characteristic name which John gives to Christ).

> "*I am come that they might have life, and that they might have it more abundantly.*"

We must always be quite clear that John never uses the word "life" in a material or physical sense: it is always that spiritual life which was in Jesus and which he imparts to believers. It is equally important to remember that when John uses the word "believe" he means something much more than intellectual assent; he means being convinced to the point of action. To believe is to accept wholeheartedly the offer of that new quality of life which is eternal. To refuse it is to reject the gift of God which He wants to give to all men through Jesus, who is himself "*The Life which is the light of men.*" Now this gift of God which John calls eternal life is not something which begins after death: it is something to be enjoyed here and now. Here again we must understand the word "death" in the sense in which John uses it. In this book and in the letters of John, "death" is not a physical happening but a spiritual condition of blindness or insensitiveness to the Light (another of John's names for Jesus is the "Light of the World"). In rejecting the gift of this quality of life which is eternal, men are turning their backs on the light and in so doing they are, as it were, pronouncing their own "death sentence." But Christians know that they have "passed out of death into Life." Why? Because they have begun to live the Eternal life of Love.

The Christian Church has not yet caught up with the thoughts which John is expressing in this "Spiritual" Gospel. In the Apostle's Creed the faithful are still invited to profess their belief in Judgment Day at the end of the world; but John is not thinking in those terms at all. For him, Judgment Day may be tomorrow, but it is just as likely to have been yesterday or today. For him, as an American writer has put it, "Judgment is not something which happens *to* us. It is something that happens *in* us. It is not some external pain God will inflict upon us, like a smarting spanking by-and-by, but an internal disruption in our souls as we re-act to good and evil and the will of Christ. (*John, the Universal Gospel*, p. 129, C. W. Quimby.)

All the seven "Signs" which John gives, from the Marriage in Cana to the Raising of Lazarus, should be read and interpreted in this spiritual sense. If it is a story of illness (the Nobleman's Son) it is a spiritual disability which is healed. If it is lameness (the Bethesda incident) it is spiritual impotence which is overcome. If it is hunger (the Feeding of the Multitude) it is spiritual hunger which is satisfied with "the Bread of Life." If Jesus walks upon the waters in the darkness of the Galilean night, it is to rescue his disciples from the moral perils and spiritual darkness of this world. If he restores health to the sick, or sight to the blind, it is spiritual insight and not simply physical sight which is gradually developed. All this is true to the account of Christ's cures in the other Gospels. He always operates directly on the *spirit* of the man or woman and leaves to God any physical effect which may or may not ensue. "Thy sins be forgiven thee" always precedes "Take up thy bed and walk." So does the challenge to the impotent man at Bethesda, "Wouldest thou be made whole?" Everything turns on the rightness or wrongness of one's spiritual attitude. Man is primarily a spiritual, not a material, being. And is not a spiritual change in a man a greater miracle than a material one?

This introduces us to the last of these seven signs, the Raising of Lazarus. This is not a story of the resuscitation of a four-day dead corpse: it is John's final picture of Christ Jesus who is himself *"the Resurrection and the Life"* (11 : 25), the giver of eternal life here and now to one who is not simply spiritually blind or ill or lame or deaf but to one who is spiritually dead, *"dead,"* as St. Paul had described people, *"in trespasses and sins."* John's concern here is not with physical death or the life beyond the grave; it is with spiritual death or "deadness" here and now—a far more terrible thing. John obviously had in mind the awful truth expressed by Jesus when he said, *"Let the dead bury their own dead: but go thou and publish the Kingdom of God"* (Luke 9: 60). One may have all one's physical faculties and yet be, as we say, "dead as a door nail."

Lazarus is clearly a man in that condition. In this great story John was trying to steer his readers between two ideas about Immortality which he believed to be false, two rocks upon which Faith may easily founder. The Jews believed in a physical resurrection *"at the last day."* This belief is expressed by Martha in the story, when Jesus says *"Thy brother shall rise again,"* and Martha replies, *"I know that he shall rise again in the Resurrection at the last day."* To this Jesus immediately replies, *"I am the Resurrection, and the Life; he that believeth in me, though he were dead* (spiritually dead), *yet shall he live: and whosoever liveth and believeth in me shall never die."* (11: 24, 25). Eternal life is a present as well as a future experience. To show that this is true and that Lazarus will not have to wait for "Eternal Life," but can have it here and now, his restoration to life takes place here and now on this earth. The Greeks on the other hand (and those Gnostics and Christians influenced by them) could not conceive of any hereafter as anything but a purely spiritual, formless and rather nebulous existence. John replies to this in the story of Lazarus by showing that the one-time "dead" soul, after he has been spiritually raised, retains his personal identity. *"He that was dead came forth."* All that has to be done for him now is to set him free from the "grave clothes" of his past "living death." *"Loose him and let him go."*

If we ask how Christ raises the spiritually dead to the quality of eternal life, John's answer is simple and direct—he did it by love. *"Now Jesus loved Martha and her sister Mary and Lazarus"* (11 : 5). But this word "love," which we use so indiscriminately in English, is a very rare and special word in Greek. Indeed, it is hardly ever found in Greek literature outside the New Testament. The commoner word is EROS (English "Erotic") or PHILIA (English "Philanthropy"), but in St. John's writings (and in St. Paul's Hymn of Love, I Corinthians 13) it is always AGAPĒ. The word is difficult to translate. At its root it means "unique" or very specially precious. So we might say that it stands for the intensest personal relationship and intimacy possible. "God is AGAPĒ" in His infinite Being, and stands in this relationship to all men. Jesus has shown or "manifested" this love of God in action, and according to John it is the distinguishing mark by which Christians are to be known.

"By this shall all men know that ye are my disciples, if ye have love one to another."

This exactly corresponds to St. Paul's great words, *"If any man have not the spirit of Christ, he is none of his."*

John brings this word Love into connection with Life (in the spiritual sense) and teaches that a man's "liveness" or "deadness" is to be measured by the quality of his love. *"We know,"* he writes (I John 3 : 14), *"that we have passed from death into life, because we love the brethren. He that loveth not his brother abideth in death."* Without this love we are "dead" to one another and there is no relationship but hostility or indifference between us. At the last supper, according to the other Gospel writers, there was an absence of love. A quarrel about precedence broke out among the disciples. John does not mention this, but simply records how Jesus changed the atmosphere by going round to each of the disciples and doing for each of them personally the most menial act of service. *"Then he poureth water into a basin, and began to wash the disciples' feet, and to wipe them with the towel wherewith he was girded"* (13 : 5). No one looking at that picture could fail to understand the real meaning of Love or doubt its power to change an atmosphere of dissension. The episode of the feet-washing is the last supreme instance during his ministry of the "love of Christ which passeth knowledge."

It prepares our minds to appreciate the point of view which John takes of Christ's death. In recording the story of the Cross and all that led up to it, John presents us with quite a different aspect from that of the other Evangelists. They give the actual history. John concentrates our attention upon its spiritual significance and actual consequences for the believer. It is indeed a "sign" or manifestation of the love of Christ. But it is something much more than this: it is an actual giving or transmission of Christ's quality of eternal life to man.

John is teaching us this all through his book by the names he gives to Jesus. He is the Good Shepherd who *"lays down his life for the sheep"*: he is also the "Door" through which the sheep may safely pass to fresh pastures (10: 9). In the other Gospels Jesus had described himself as the "Sower" who sows the Word of God in men's hearts: but here he calls himself the "Seed" which must "die" if it is to bear fruit.

"Except a grain of wheat fall into the ground and die, it abideth alone; but if it die, it bringeth forth much fruit" (12: 24).

That is the answer which Jesus sends to the Greeks who wanted to see him. By it he is implying that men will have to wait to see the full significance and meaning of his life until after it has borne fruit in those for whom he has laid down that life and in whom his quality of eternal life will be evident. Men will see the "grace" in our lives which flows from his love (1: 16).

From John's point of view, the death of the Cross is not something done to Jesus: it is something which he himself "accomplishes" as the will of his Father. Indeed it is his greatest accomplishment.

"Therefore doth my Father love me, because I lay down my life, that I may take it again. No man taketh it from me, but I lay it down of myself. I have power to lay it down, and I have power to take it again. This commandment have I received of my Father" (10: 17–18).

The Cross becomes for St. John Christ's crowning Act of Love. All the way through this Gospel Jesus has been shown giving himself to people. Nicodemus, the woman of Samaria, the man born blind, and most clearly Martha, Mary and Lazarus, are each given his whole interest and concern. He "loves" (AGAPĒ) them all into the new life. Each of them passes "out of death into life"—most dramatically Lazarus. For each of them Christianity is, as the historian Von Harnack has described it, "Eternal life here and now under the eyes and in the strength of God." But it is through his death on the Cross that this self-giving is completed and Eternal Life (Christ's own quality of life) is now available to all whom he "draws unto himself." That is why he can say with his last breath, "*It is finished*" (19 : 30). The Greek word used (TETE-LESTAI) really means fulfilment, accomplishment, bringing to perfection or maturity.

No one but John has recorded this as the final word from the Cross. I do not think it is historic in the sense that these words actually passed the lips of Jesus. But John carries us beyond literal into spiritual history. Dr. Charles Raven helps us here. He writes, "If by history we mean the interpretation of personality by one who has pondered over the significance of events and reflected and explained them, then this Gospel will stand pre-eminent." (*Jesus and the Gospel of Love*, p. 226.)

It is important to notice that Jesus (according to Matthew) used the same word (TELEIOS) in the Sermon on the Mount: "*Ye shall therefore be perfect, even as your Father which is in heaven is perfect*" (Matthew 5: 48). These words have often been a stumbling-block. People have naturally said, "We're none of us perfect, and never will be: the thing is impossible." John has shown throughout his Gospel how perfection, full maturity, is possible to all who believe that Jesus through his life and especially through his death gives men "*power to become*" what, unaided by his grace, they could never otherwise be. This would be his answer to anyone who says that all we need is the ethics of the Sermon on the Mount. We must have the spiritual oxygen of the grace of Christ to enable us to ascend even the lower slopes and to follow even the first steps of his most holy life.

Finally, we notice that it is John alone who shows that it was because of the intense quality of this grace or love-relationship which existed between Jesus and his closest friends that they became convinced of the fact of his Resurrection. Jesus had lifted them so far beyond what may be apprehended by the five senses, into the sphere of spiritual perception, that they were able to see him in his Risen state. Physical death had only temporarily obscured or impaired the spiritual relationship which Jesus had built up between himself and them. It was to Mary Magdalene, whose sins were forgiven "because she loved much" that the Risen Lord first was able to make himself known. It was to Simon Peter, whose love had outlasted his temporary failure and denial, that Jesus came as the mists of the night of frustration rolled away.

"And in the morning, Jesus stood upon the shore."

But this triumph of the "love divine, all loves excelling" is specially and dramatically shown in the case of Thomas. In his case "hope and fear . . . is just our chance of the prize of learning love," as Browning says. Thomas has come down to us with the adjective "doubting" attached to his name. But that is a total misrepresentation of his true character. Doubt is no sin. It is often the gateway to belief.

> "There lives more faith in honest doubt,
> Believe me, than in half the Creeds."

Thomas is just an ordinary average man. He is the "plain" man who wants to think things out and find things out for himself and will not readily accept other people's stories, not even the evidence of his best friends. Such a man, who was not prepared to accept things that Jesus said just because He said them, was specially dear to the Master who challenged people to "judge for themselves what is right." To Thomas, as to many another plain man in our own time, some of the stories which the other disciples told of the Resurrection were unacceptable. They were either too vague or else too realistic. To Thomas's mind there could be only two alternatives: either the body of the Risen Lord was physical, and therefore actually visible and tangible, or else it was invisible and intangible, in fact a phantom (as the Gnostics said).

So St. John uses the experience of Thomas to steer his readers between these two false views, just as he had already done in presenting the truth about Eternal Life. What led Thomas to the truth was not a physical nor was it a purely spiritual experience. It was something in between the two. It happened in that part of man where the physical and the spiritual actually meet. It happened in his mind. When the Risen Lord came into the Upper Room *"when the doors were shut"* (which rules out the physical), the thing that convinced Thomas that Jesus was no phantom was that the Master showed him that he still knew, as of old, all that had been going on in his disciple's mind. Jesus named the very test which Thomas himself had been thinking about all the past week. He was the same Jesus who "knew their thoughts" and read men like a book.

> So Jesus said, *"Reach hither thy finger, and see my hands; and reach hither thy hand and put it into my side: and be not faithless, but believing"* (20: 27).

Those words "Be not faithless" are the key to the understanding of the story. If there had been something there which Thomas could actually see with his eyes or touch with his hand, no faith whatever would have been necessary. Faith would have been lost in sight and he would have been able to say, "Seeing is believing." As it was, it was exactly the equivalent and more than the equivalent of seeing. Thomas "saw" and "touched," as we have to, not by hand or eye but by faith. And this faith by which he came to full belief called forth the last beatitude with which the Gospel ends, *"Blessed are they that have not seen, and yet have believed."*

> "O world invisible, we view thee,
> O world intangible, we touch thee,
> O world unknowable, we know thee,
> Inapprehensible, we clutch thee!"

Yes, but that is a perennial difficulty to the plain man represented in the Gospel by Thomas. Indeed it is a difficulty which must always be faced so long as we are incarnate in matter. It will always be hard to believe that the unseen is more real than the seen, so long as we are in a body of flesh and blood. It will always be felt that the visible presence of Jesus nineteen centuries ago in Palestine was more real than his spiritual presence in the heart of the believer. That accounts for the tenacity with which people have always held on to a literal belief in what is known as "the second coming." This was a matter which seems to have greatly troubled some people in the Church at Ephesus in the days of John. So long as any of the original disciples of Jesus remained alive, there had persisted the primitive belief based on a literal interpretation of words attributed to Jesus which suggested that he would "come again" in glory to set up the Messianic Kingdom of God on earth. John would be familiar with words of Jesus reported by St. Mark, which actually seemed to lend colour to the idea that this return of Christ in glory would take place in the lifetime of that generation which had known him in the flesh. "*There be some of them that stand here which shall not taste of death till they have seen the kingdom of God come with power*" (Mark 9: 1).

The earlier letters of St. Paul (especially 1 and 2 Thessalonians) show that even he himself may at an early stage of his spiritual development have held some such belief. But he warned his converts not to get so pre-occupied with that expectation as to lose interest in the ordinary affairs of life. His later letters (Colossians and Philippians) show that Paul's own thought on that subject had undergone a development. He had seen that the Lord had indeed returned already in a spiritual instead of a material manner, in the hearts and minds of believers. "*This is my prayer*," he wrote to the Ephesians, "*that Christ may dwell in your hearts by faith*" (3: 17).

Some scholars think that "Ephesians" was not actually written by St. Paul, but it is certainly Pauline in thought. The fact is that by the end of the first century this true thought of the Christ Spirit dwelling in the heart of the Christian had begun to establish itself among the more thinking people in the Church. But, as we know, the faith of the ordinary rank and file always lags behind, and those who have neither time nor inclination to think deeply will often pin their faith, sometimes their whole faith, upon an outmoded belief such as this. I'm afraid it must be admitted, especially with regard to the "Second Coming," that the Church in its Creeds and many of its prayers (see Advent Collects) has encouraged people to continue to cherish the literal rather than the more spiritual form of this belief. Here again, is not the Spiritual experience of the indwelling Christ a greater thing than any material event?

Now we can be sure that the author of the Fourth Gospel was acutely aware of this. About the year A.D. 100 (which must be the approximate date of this book) it is just possible that there may have been two people still living who had seen Jesus in the flesh, John the "beloved disciple" and John the Elder, our Author. If therefore they both died before the Lord returned, the simple faith of many would receive a staggering blow. That is the best reason that one can give for two very striking features which are unique in the Fourth Gospel—The Discourses (14–17), and the 21st chapter, which is obviously a sort of appendix to the whole work. Those farewell discourses which John sets in the framework of his account of the Last Supper (which significantly does not contain any reference to the words of Institution) are full of references to the coming of the Holy Spirit, the Comforter. Christ promises that the Spirit (whom Paul had identified with the Spirit of Christ himself), when he comes, will make all his teaching crystal clear to Christians (14: 25ff.; 16: 8–14). In writing this, John obviously had in mind the illumination of the Apostles at Pentecost and their subsequent recognition, frequently mentioned in the Acts of the Apostles, that *"the Spirit of Jesus"* was the directive power of their lives (Acts 8: 29, 16: 7). He hoped that his readers would see for themselves from this that Christ's words about "coming again" must now be understood spiritually. To make doubly sure, John appended Chapter 21 to his book.

He uses the story, probably derived from the original ending of St. Mark (which has perished) of the first post-Resurrection meeting of the Sons of Zebedee and Simon Peter with Jesus at the Sea of Galilee when they had been out fishing all night and had caught nothing. But there are two other very interesting men there in John's story—the two men who had been what we should call "doubtful starters," Thomas, and Nathaniel of Cana in Galilee (he it was who on first hearing of Jesus had said, "Can any good thing come out of Nazareth?"). It is to them and to Simon Peter who had thrice denied his Lord that the Risen Master comes, not as literal-minded people were expecting (upon the clouds of heaven in glory), but as a fish-hawker on the familiar shore of Galilee in the mists of morning. "*In the morning, Jesus stood upon the shore.*" "That," says John, who had watched so many people's "Second-Advent" hopes fade in the light of common day, "that is the manner of his coming; and I know that it is a *real* coming, and that all I have written in my book is, like that coming, a spiritual reality." Furthermore, nobody must go on building up false hopes about any visible return of Christ so long as any of the original disciples remain alive. He says that very strongly, through the conversation near the end.

> "*Peter seeing him* (the beloved disciple) *saith to Jesus, Lord, and what shall this man do? Jesus saith unto him, If I will that he tarry till I come, what is that to thee? Follow thou me. Then went this saying abroad among the brethren, that that disciple should not die: yet Jesus said not unto him, He shall not die; but, if I will that he tarry till I come, what is that to thee?*"

"*What is that to thee? Follow thou me.*" The question and the command might be applied to the thousand and one out-moded beliefs which have obstructed the plain path of Christian discipleship through the centuries. The questions, "How did he come?" or "How will he come?" are superseded by the good news proclaimed by this greatest of all biblical writers in a dozen different ways, that the Son of God *has* come and has given us a new understanding of the Father.

The questions, "What did he do?" "What did he reveal?" are superseded by the promise that through the Spirit which Christ has breathed into the world there are yet greater works that he is doing and will do, and yet more luminous revelations of Truth which the world is not yet able to receive. "*I have yet many things to say unto you but ye cannot bear them now.*"

The question, "If a man die, shall he live again?" which has always been treated as a purely speculative and rather unpractical question, becomes in this Gospel a personal challenge, "Have you got the quality of eternal life abiding and maturing in your soul?" For just as the body is dead without the soul to animate it, so the soul is in darkness without the flame of the Spirit to kindle and enlighten it. What the sun is to the planets in the Solar System, Christ is to the souls of men. "*I am the light of the world; he that followeth me shall not walk in darkness but shall have the light of life.*"

The questions, "Where shall we worship?" or "How shall we worship?" which have divided men into a hundred warring sects and even today confuse and baffle many a Thomas or Nathaniel with denominational differences, are transcended and must one day be obliterated by the sublime affirmation:

> "*Believe me, the hour cometh when neither in this mountain nor yet in Jerusalem shall ye worship the Father . . . God is Spirit, and they that worship him must worship him in Spirit and in Truth.*"

"*The hour cometh.*" Does John leave us with nothing more than a distant hope, a dream of the remote future when these things shall come to pass? That is where all the prophets had had to leave it. But John shows us that Jesus is more than a prophet. He does not simply say, "the hour cometh," or, "these things shall be": he adds three luminous words, "AND NOW IS." This is his greater work. He brings the distant future into the living present. He is indeed the Creative Word of the Father.

The glorious spiritual future of a Christ-enlightened earth when men shall live in truth under the direct inspiration of God is already here in the womb of the present. "The world's great Age begins anew" every time that one more soul is "*born from above*" and awakens, through listening to the voice of him who is the Resurrection and the Life, to his true destiny which is a life that never ends. It begins here; it "*now is*": it will be perfected hereafter in the further reaches of the Spiritual Universe which Jesus familiarly calls "*My Father's house.*"

CHAPTER FIFTEEN

Travellers in Eternity

*"Here we have no abiding city, but our citizenship
is in heaven"*

PEOPLE are always asking us Christian ministers what we think of Spiritualism. For answer I would always refer them to the Bible. In the literature of the Old Testament we have the story of King Saul and the "woman which had a familiar spirit" (i.e. a medium) at Endor (I Sam. 28), and the warnings of Isaiah, the prophet of the eighth century, *"When they tell you to consult mediums and ghosts that cheep and gibber in low murmurs, ask them if a nation should not rather consult its God. Say, 'Why consult the dead on behalf of the living? Consult the message and the counsel of God'"* (Isa. 8: 19). In the New Testament we have Christ's famous story of Dives and Lazarus which ends with words which we may take as his judgment upon the value of psychic phenomena as contrasted with spiritual wisdom.

"They have Moses and the Prophets: let them hear them . . . If they hear not Moses and the Prophets, neither will they be persuaded though one rose from the dead" (Luke 16: 29–31).

Spiritualism as practised today has its antecedents in remote antiquity. The narrative of King Saul and the Witch of Endor has preserved in some detail an exact description of the kind of thing that is going on in countless séances up and down the country at this very moment. Here is a man at the end of his tether resorting to a practice which, as King of Israel, he had officially denounced and forbidden by law.

"Now Saul had cleared the mediums and wizards out of the country" (I Sam. 28: 3).

But in a personal dilemma Saul wondered, as many more have done, whether after all he could get some comfort from it. So we find him disguising himself and going to a medium, for that is the modern equivalent of the phrase "a woman that hath a familiar spirit." A "familiar spirit" is what we call a "control," a control being a discarnate intelligence who, like a telephone operator on a switch board, puts you through to the spirit with whom you desire to communicate. Now King Saul had one person above all others in the unseen world with whom at the crisis of his life he desired to communicate—Samuel to whom he owed his elevation to the throne; and Samuel had recently died. So we are not surprised to find that when the medium asks whom he wishes her to "call up," Saul asks for his old friend and counsellor. "*And he said, bring me up Samuel.*" The medium, whose telepathic powers are by this time in full operation, recognises the sitter. "*You are Saul!*" she cries in alarm. Saul reassures her that she shall not be punished for transgressing his own anti-spiritualist legislation.

Samuel immediately "comes through" and appears to be very much annoyed. "*Why have you disturbed me by bringing me up?*" I should take those words to be accounted for, in part at any rate, by the medium's telepathic rapport with Saul's guilty conscience. And the message that purported to come through from Samuel may be accounted for in the same way. In any case it was of little or no value. All that Samuel's message did for Saul was to confirm his worst fears. He was told that he was going to his doom.

But is it always so? Do not thousands of people derive great comfort from thus contacting their friends and loved ones on the other side? Undoubtedly they do. But who is to say how much of it actually comes from the friend who is supposed to be communicating? Our knowledge of our own minds, particularly of our sub-conscious minds revealed by psychology, forces this question upon us. Everybody knows how suggestible the subconscious mind is, and the evidence accumulated by the Society of Psychical Research (quite different from Spiritualism because it is highly scientific in its methods and techniques) has made telepathic communication a certain fact. Therefore any message purporting to come from the other world is bound to be coloured, if not actually framed, by subconscious thoughts both of the medium and the recipient. I believe in the sincerity of many mediums, but I should always have mental reservations about their ability to communicate a message unadulterated by their own subconscious thoughts. As an infantry officer it was my duty to train men to pass a message down the line. Any one who has tried that experiment will know how different the message is by the time it has passed through fifty or sixty *conscious* minds. I remember experimenting once with this simple message, "The Captain's horse has got rheumatism." When I collected it at the end of the line it had become, "The Captain can't be on parade to-day because he's got rheumatism through sitting on a wet saddle!" If that kind of thing can happen to a message which has been passed through *conscious* minds, how much greater are chances of adulteration when it has passed through *subconscious* minds. In addition to that, don't forget that the average "Sitter" or recipient at a private séance or a public meeting is usually in an emotional and therefore highly suggestible state of mind. Further, we all know the power of atmosphere and the sense of mystery which attends all these experiments. I believe that even the most unsusceptible, and even sceptical, listener will find it difficult not to be impressed by the half-crown fortune-teller at a fair.

Rudyard Kipling seems to have been well aware of all this, when he wrote his poem "Endor."

> "Even so, we have need of faith
> And patience to follow the clue.
> Often, at first, what the dear one saith
> Is babble or jest or untrue.
> Lying spirits perplex us sore,
> Till our loves and our lives
> Are well-known at Endor.
>
> Oh, the road to Endor is the oldest road
> And the craziest road of all!
> Straight runs it down to the witch's abode
> As it did in the days of Saul.
> And nothing has changed of the sorrow in store
> For such as go down on the road to Endor."

He also mentions the unreliability of the Control, which he calls the "hireling," and complains that:

> "The son must send word to the mother that bore
> Through an hireling's mouth.
> 'Tis the rule of Endor."

Must we then give up the whole idea of contact or communication with our friends who have passed into the Other World? I do not believe that mankind will ever abandon the attempt, whether the Churches recognise it or not. My chief reason for believing this is that there is a great deal of evidence from the experience of people—and they are not necessarily professing Christians—that their friends on the other side are helping, guiding and strengthening them all through their earthly lives. This I have learnt chiefly from people who know that their own death is imminent. To some, the presence of a departed friend or relative will often come as a complete surprise; to others it has been for a long time a perfectly natural experience, so natural and yet to them so holy and so precious that they have not spoken of it. I should never presume to doubt the validity of their experience.

But these experiences differ from the phenomena of spiritualism in one very important respect. They are not *sought*: they are given. They are not brought about by any earthly agency like a medium; they seem quite clearly to be blessings from Above. It is our friends and kinsfolk in the larger life who take the initiative and responsibility of contacting us, not we them. Here I believe the hymn is right which runs,

> "Saints departed even thus
> Hold communion still with us;
> Still with us beyond the veil,
> Praying, pleading without fail."

Is not this getting it the right way round? Remember Kipling's warning,

> "Lying spirits perplex us sore,
> Till our loves and our lives
> Are well-known at Endor."

I have no doubt that there is a kind of slum in the very near "here-after" in which there may dwell myriads of infantile, childish, and even wicked spirits who left the earth spiritually undeveloped and are still earthbound like the unclean spirit which Jesus described as "wandering through desolate places, seeking rest." Supposing one of these should succeed in cutting in and get through the medium, pretending to be your friend. There are cases on record in which this has been proved. So I should never reach my hand through the veil but should leave it to God to give me guidance or help through whatever agency His wisdom may ordain. Very likely God will guide you through some departed friend who was your guide and counsellor in the earth life, or some higher spirit with whom you have a spiritual affinity.

Now all that is very far from being mere speculation. The Old Testament supplied us with the experience of King Saul and the Witch of Endor. The New Testament presents us with Jesus and the Spirits of Moses and Elijah, who were his great spiritual predecessors when on earth and therefore his most likely spiritual friends and helpers in the other world. Look for a moment at the situation described in St. Luke 9.

Jesus had just been trying to share with his disciples the grim prospect of failure, rejection, suffering and his probably early death. They remonstrated with him and Jesus could not induce them to discuss it. So in utter loneliness he took Peter, James and John, his most intimate friends into a mountain hoping no doubt to talk further with them so that they might learn to walk with death as he himself was learning to do. And out there under the stars, Jesus experienced what we have come to call the Communion of Saints.

"*As he was praying, there talked with him two men, which were Moses and Elijah, who appeared in glory.*"

Notice here that it happened "*as he was praying.*" Jesus was not praying to Moses and Elijah, neither was he seeking contact with them. He was praying to his heavenly Father. He was bringing to God his burden of loneliness; he was like the Psalmist letting God "know his soul in adversity." He may quite possibly have meditated upon the loneliness and spiritual frustration of his great spiritual predecessors, Moses and Elijah, and as he did so, he may have begun to feel that he was in good company. Had not Moses in many a desperate moment regretted that God had chosen him for an impossible task? Had not Elijah in an agony of loneliness prayed that he might die? And then he found that in actual fact Moses and Elijah were there, not of course in the flesh, but "in glory," that is, in the spirit. And Moses gave to Jesus what would appear to be a very important clue to his identity. We are told that *"they spake with him of his death and departure which he should accomplish at Jerusalem."*

In the Authorised Version the word is "decease." That is a very bad rendering of the Greek word, which is not the usual THANATOS—death—but the most unusual word EXODOS which means "a way out" or "a way through." But more than that, this word Exodos, or Exodus, had historical associations with the Exodus of the Children of Israel from Egypt into the Promised Land. And it was of course Moses who had personally led it.

So it was that when he was in prayer there was imparted to the listening soul of Jesus two great truths which were necessary for him and are even more necessary for us.

At the outset of his career Jesus had meditated on the saying that Man can only live his true life by listening to every word that proceedeth out of the mouth of God. Here, as he faces loneliness, he is assured that he is not alone but in the glorious company of the prophets which were before him. Here, as he faces death, man's last enemy, he is assured that it is not a "No Entry" but an Exodus, a through way into the Promised Land.

> "And death is but a covered way that leadeth into light,
> Wherein no blinded child can stray out of the Father's sight."

Christianity entered Europe as the good news or Gospel of Eternal Life. Our pre-occupation with material concerns has led us to assume that man *can* live by bread alone. But our present dilemma into which we have been led by that materialistic assumption challenges us once again to recognise that spiritual order which over-arches and interpenetrates our physical being. What we need, therefore, is a truly Christian spiritualism like that of Christ himself, who went to the Father in prayer and was granted the help and encouragement and guidance of kindred spirits who had trod the earthly road before him and now returned to inspire him with the knowledge that he was greatly attended all the way and that, just as birth is our entrance into the world of matter, so death is but birth into that world of Spirit which is our Eternal Home.

CHAPTER SIXTEEN

The Bible and Human Needs

Can the Bible really speak to Modern Man? Is the message of its authors relevant to life in the twentieth century? Can we claim with the Collect for the second Sunday in Advent that it is really "written for our learning"?

Well, as we have seen in the preceding chapters, the Bible is not the kind of book to which you can refer a question and expect to get a direct or definite answer. Treated in that way it can do, as it often has done, more harm than good. But if you go to it as you would to a greatly revered teacher, or approach it as you would a great picture by one of the Old Masters and, following the suggestion of that Collect, not only read it, but "inwardly disgest it," then you will find that it can do the same kind of thing for you that the teacher or the painting can do, and that is to give you the right approach to the problems of life, if not to life itself. For however widely we may differ from one another in our interpretations of the vastly various books of the Bible—many of which we have not space enough even to mention in a book of this size— there are certain fundamental human needs which are more fully satisfied here than in any other collection of literature. This is because the message of the Bible comes to us through great men and women, through its authors and the supreme personalities whom they bring before us.

God is always speaking to man in different ways; through Nature, which is His living garment; through History, in which discerning writers have been able to read something of His purposes for the human race; but most clearly of all through those who have begun to subdue Nature around them and within and have been the makers of history not so much by what they did as by what they were. That is the verdict of the unknown author of the "Epistle to Hebrews," rendered by Mr. J. B. Phillips as follows: "*God who gave to our forefathers many different glimpses of the truth in the words of the prophets, has now at the end of the present age given us the Truth in the Son."*

How does God speak through a man? Not so much through anything he does, through any particular truth that he teaches, as through what he is—his personality. History has made us familiar with the great deeds of national and political heroes and leaders like Caesar, Napoleon or Charlemagne. Literature has preserved for us the great fundamental truths given to the world by Socrates or Shakespeare. But the Bible introduces us to a kind of leadership different from that of the statesman or the philosopher—the leadership of the Man of God, the Saint. That is why the Bible is so relevant to the needs of every man in every age, and particularly to our own. It is not a book for specialists in any particular field, but for "the wayfaring man," the common man, the plain man, the man in the street. His great task is not to subdue nations or to sway the masses, although he may be "some village Hampden" or even "a mute inglorious Milton," but to keep his head on the edge of the precipices and to keep a good heart in the sloughs of despond which he must encounter between the cradle and the grave. It is for these emergencies as well as for the more humdrum paths of life that the ordinary man needs the leadership and the contributions which men like Abraham and Moses, Joshua and David, Elijah and Hosea, Peter and Paul, and above all the Master himself, have to offer him. These are the leaders for him, the Saints.

Now a Saint is not (as stained-glass windows have caricatured him) a feeble, effeminate, nerveless creature who couldn't say boo to a goose, nor a flaccid anaemic figure waiting with folded hands for a miracle, but one who, being himself more aware of the presence of God than of anything else, is always making others aware of God. The Saint, as Dr. Phillips Brooks used to say, is not part of the "soft-padding of the Universe," but a link in the "strong chain of God's presence in humanity running down through all history." The true Saints of God, including Jesus Christ, may have had miracles attributed to them in ages predisposed to the miraculous which we cannot and do not wish to accept, but nothing, however grotesque or bizarre, which has come to be associated with their names, can ever wholly obscure from us the miracles that they were. It is this distinct thing about them which meets our commonest needs and speaks to our common humanity. It is because the great men of the Bible were characterised by this quality of real saintliness that God can still speak those strong words by which a man can "live his life courageously." Courage, Patience, Comfort, Hope! What more do we want than these? And who of us can hope to get along without them?

We are being taught by the frustrations and the spiritual bankruptcy of our times that man, however rich he may become in *things*, may yet be so poor in soul that he cannot cope with them, and that he cannot afford to take a single step without heeding every word that comes to him from the Wisdom and the Love that created him in its own image and for the ultimate fulfilment of purposes beyond all his materialistic dreams. Man, as Darwin said, may bear in his body the indelible marks of his humble origin, but he bears at the same time in his soul potentialities and capacities for

> "Ends he has not wrought for,
> Good he has not sought for,
> Goals he has not fought for,
> By Love that never dies."

All this he bears in his soul or personality. But none of these spiritual ends, none of these spiritual goals, nothing of that true goodness can be achieved by his personality, but only by the Spirit of God *through* that personality.

We must never lose sight of the original meanings of that great word. "Persona" in Latin, like its opposite number "prosōpon" in Greek, originally meant the actor's mask *through which* (per) he "sounded" or spoke. Then it came to mean the part which he played upon the stage (hence your theatre programmes still speak of the characters in the play, dramatis personae), and so in the days when the Creeds were in process of formulation the part or rôle which God or man plays upon the stage of history.

Our dilemma is often recognised today when it is said that what